PERSONALITY MIRROR TRANSFORMS YOU

REFLECT, REALIGN, RISE

Unveil the Layers Of Personality, Turn Reflection into Reinvention, See Who You Are, and Shape Who You Become

Jayaprakash Nagathihalli

Transformation Mentor

Personality Mirror Transforms You

A Book on

UNVEILING THE LAYERS OF PERSONALITY

TURN REFLECTION INTO REINVENTION

SEE WHO YOU ARE, SHAPE WHO YOU BECOME

REFLECT, REALIGN, RISE

Written by Jayaprakash Nagathihalli

Illustrations: Sharanu Chetti

FOREWARD BY
Dr. BHARATH CHANDRA

During the search for Sita, Hanuman and other monkey warriors were deeply worried about how to cross the vast ocean and how to set foot in Lanka. At that time, Jambavanta, the elderly among them, reminded Hanuman of something everyone now knows as a timeless truth.

You are the son of Vayu (the wind god), blessed by the gods. You can assume any form at will. You have the ability to travel through the skies with the speed of thought. If anyone among the monkey warriors can go to Lanka quickly, it is you.

Hanuman, who had been sitting quietly in a corner thinking of himself as just an ordinary being with no special power, was suddenly inspired by Jambavanta's words. Courage replaced his doubt. In a flash, he prepared himself, leapt into the sky along the path of the wind, reached Lanka, met Sita, challenged Ravana and Indrajit, and set the entire golden Lanka ablaze with the fire from his tail.

Now, if you're wondering why Dr. Bharat Chandra, while speaking about personality development, is talking so much about Hanuman and Jambavanta it's not without reason. At first glance, it may seem unrelated, but if you look deeper, you'll realise that we are all, in some way, like Hanuman in our real lives.

Despite being immensely powerful and capable, and having all the blessings, we often suffer like ordinary people, unaware of our own strengths. We possess the power and capacity to face many challenges and situations, but not realising it, we hesitate and shrink. Though extraordinary, we live like we are ordinary. Without using our intellect, ability, or willpower, we let our lives slip by.

Hanuman was very mischievous as a child. Blessed by the gods, he used to be proud and disruptive, especially during rituals conducted by sages. As a result, one sage cursed him, causing him to forget his own powers. Only when someone reminded him, would he become aware of his true strength.

This same issue affects us too; we are unaware of our own abilities. It is only when someone inspires or reminds us that we discover our real potential. This is precisely what Jayaprakash Nagathihalli has been doing for ages. Those who attend his personality development workshops emerge transformed, like new Hanumans. They move toward goals they had once ignored or believed impossible. After participating, they race ahead in life and achieve previously unimaginable levels of success. Ask Nagathihalli, and he can share hundreds of such stories and examples.

To those who ask, What will I gain from attending a personality development workshop? I can offer this analogy for better clarity:

One day, I ask you to run. You stop after 3 kilometres. I ask you again, and you manage 1 more kilometre before stopping. I encourage you once more, and despite your reluctance, you push through another kilometre before declaring, I can't go any further. I'm out of breath. My physical strength has reached its limit.

Then something amazing happens. You turn around and notice a giant, ferocious tiger chasing you. Instantly, without even thinking, you run another 3 kilometres!

Just moments ago, you said it was impossible to run, that you couldn't take even a single step. But upon seeing the tiger behind you, you unknowingly ran another 3 kilometres in an instant!

In English, we refer to this phenomenon as First Wind and Second Wind. You believed all the air in your lungs was exhausted, but when you saw the tiger, you tapped into your *Second Wind.* It's a hidden system within us that activates without our conscious awareness.

This is exactly what you tap into after attending a personality development workshop. Whatever you are today, whatever success you've achieved, you believe that is your full potential. You've drawn a boundary around what you consider your maximum capability. But when you fully immerse yourself in a personality development program, those boundaries shift. Symbolically, you access the *Second Wind* within you. You rise higher than you ever imagined possible.

Having conducted these workshops for over four decades and having seen lakhs of people transform, there's no doubt that Mr. Nagathihalli has had the same experience.

To those who skeptically ask, What change can a few days of personality development bring in me? this should serve as a clear example.

To see transformation in a person, sometimes one single moment is enough. That moment may happen in a Hanuman temple, while reading a book, in a conversation with a mentor, or in a personality development workshop. No one can change someone else. We must invite that moment of transformation into ourselves.

Defining life goals, developing leadership qualities, mastering communication and public speaking, managing time and mental stress effectively all of these can take us toward our highest potential.

Let me share a peculiar experience I've had. Many people who attended personality development workshops have gone on to achieve massive success in the following days, months, or years when compared to their peers. It feels like they've pressed the fast-forward button in life!

One of the greatest outcomes of personality development workshops is the defining of your life goals. If you don't have a goal, you might end up reaching something and falsely believing that is your ultimate goal. People without clear goals usually end up working for those who have them.

For example, when I had no goals, I worked *in* a school. But once I developed a grand vision, I *became* a school, and others worked *for* me. Many people say, I already know my goals, but based on decades of experience, I can tell you most are likely referring only to financial goals. Real goal-setting must extend across all the areas of life. You cannot build strength by only exercising one arm.

We must aim for holistic growth. The six key areas of life to set goals in are:

1. Personal,

2. Financial,

3. Family,

4. Intellectual,

5. Social, and

6. Spiritual.

Only goals encompassing all these domains can bring a balanced life this is the opinion of the wise.

In childhood, I read the Bhagavad Gita. I thought I understood it. I read it again in my youth and a new meaning emerged. Now, reading it in this stage of life, it reveals yet another layer of understanding. The same Gita offers different meanings depending on your life stage and level of awareness. Similarly, what you gain from a personality development program depends on where you are in life when you attend it. You will absorb and apply it according to your stage.

In youth, financial goals may seem like everything. But as you mature, you may come to value social, spiritual, and intellectual goals just as much. In my opinion, every Indian must attend such a workshop at least once. I believe Mr. Nagathihalli would wholeheartedly agree.

Jayaprakash Nagathihalli is a rare gem. A proud son of India, he has beautifully distilled the many dimensions of personality development for his students. To say he is a unique and remarkable individual would not be an exaggeration.

I express my gratitude to him for giving me the opportunity to write the foreword to *Personality Mirror Transforms you.* May God bless him with immense health, longevity, and prosperity. I hope that millions of readers benefit from this book.

Dr. Bharat Chandra

Internationally Acclaimed Trainer

Author's Note

Dear Readers,

The phrase 'Personality Mirror' is close to my heart. I strongly believe that self-awareness about our personality can only be achieved by reflecting on ourselves, just as we do in a mirror. With this belief, I have used this book as a platform to elaborate on six key aspects of personality development:

1. Physical Personality
2. Mental Personality
3. Intellectual Personality
4. Emotional Personality
5. Spiritual Personality
6. Financial Personality

To explore these aspects, I have incorporated interviews with experts for Chandana TV and specialists in various fields, including:

- Sadhana Kaikini, TVN Murthy, Mohammed Anwar
- V.R. Satyanarayana
- Mahacharya Ravi Shankar
- Shrilatha
- Guru Bhagwan
- Arjun Devayya

Additionally, a special article from financial mentor Shankar Kulkarni has been adopted from my Jayaprakash Nagathihalli YouTube channel. I have also included insights from the

Nagamma Foundation's video on 'Positive Attitude' and discussions from a few online training sessions.

Previously Published Books in Kannada:

1. Nudigannadi (Mirror of Words)
2. Fear Not Failures
3. Inferiority Complex? Why? How?
4. Celebrate Every Moment
5. Employment Skills
6. Understanding Turning Points
7. Discover Your Uniqueness
8. Sadhakara Chandana (Achiever's Achievements)
9. Sahitya Chandana (Literature)
10. Vyaktitva Chandana (Personality)
11. Nirupane Nirupisi (Mastering Presentation Skills)
12. Jeevanotsaha (Enthusiasm for Life)
13. Vyaktitwa Darpana
14. Vyaaktitwa Chandana
15. Lifu Nandene
16. Tarabetiya Takattu

Books in English:

1. Fear Not Failures
2. Inferiority Complex
3. Celebrate Every Moment
4. Transform your Life Instantly
5. Unlock the power of Uniqueness

After receiving overwhelming support for our previous books, I am delighted to present this book to you. Many readers have provided valuable feedback through letters, emails, and phone calls, which has motivated me further.

30 Years in Personality Development Field

Over the past 30 years, I have been actively involved in personality development training, reaching more than 10 lakh individuals. In the last five years, I have also expanded into online training to connect with more people. Social media has played a significant role in spreading our philosophy, and seeing individuals succeed under our guidance has been truly rewarding.

Your Feedback Matters!

I encourage you to read this book completely and share your thoughts. For online or offline training and guidance, feel free to contact us.

Bangalore
📞 Jayaprakash Nagathihalli – 9886081188

For Suggestions & Queries:

📞 Office Numbers: 9341259267, 9620303000
✉ Email: smilingjp@gmail.com
🔍 Find me on social media: *Jayaprakash Nagathihalli*

YouTube Channels:

1. Jayaprakash Nagathihalli
2. Transformation Unlimited

Contents

Foreward By Dr. Bharath Chandra II

Author's Note VIII

1. Personality Mirror 1

2. Personality Development – A Ladder to Life 7

    2A Personality Development 14

3. The Mental Mirror 30

    3A. A Discussion on the Conscious Mind in an
Online Class 36

    3B. The Power of the Subconscious Mind 41

    3C. The Super Concious Mind: A Path to Your Growth 54

    3D. Open Mind vs. Closed Mind 59

4. Intellectual Mirror 64

    4A. Problem Solving 69

    4B. Analytical Capability 75

    4C. Elevate and Uplift 81

5. Emotional Mirror 101

    5A. Emotions 107

    5B. Mother's Love 121

6. Spiritual Mirror 141

    6A. Spirituality 151

    6B. A Positive Attitude 166

7. FINANCIAL MIRROR 173

    7A. Money Management 182

    7B. STOCK MARKET 187

    7C. Earn Love, Respect, Relationships, and Experiences Along with Money 194

    7D. SPEAK TO GET RICH 200

8. Physical Mirror 217

    8A. Personality Development Through Sports 221

9. Moving into Action 235

10. Towards Balance 237

11. MENTORING - The Light of Guidance 241

About The Author 247

Disclaimer 254

1.

Personality Mirror

Telling it as it is...

The Silent Guru - The Mirror

- Jayaprakash Nagathihalli

Role of Self-Awareness

The message "Know Yourself" is of utmost importance. SWOT Analysis (Strengths, Weaknesses, Opportunities & Threats)

is truly an extremely effective tool.

- Enhance your strengths
- Transform your weaknesses into strengths
- Identify opportunities
- Overcome threats

The Book 'Nudigannadi'

Our first book, *Nudigannadi*, was an attempt to hold a mirror to words. It personally helped us a lot and enabled many readers to become excellent speakers. A mirror is an effective tool to learn speech. Don't you think the words 'Kannada' and 'Kannadi' (mirror) are quite similar?

A mirror never complains and always helps us improve our preparation. It even aids in enhancing body language. If we hold a mirror to both our inner and outer personality, wouldn't our life transform completely?

TV Show on Chandana

We successfully presented around 106 episodes under the title *Personality Mirror* on Chandana TV.

Hosting one-hour episodes on 106 different topics with 106 experts every week was an unforgettable experience. It was like living with each topic for a week. These 106 topics and experts have had a deep impact on us.

Additionally, through the *Belagu* program, we introduced over 1,200 achievers from various fields. It felt as if we traveled through many different lives. In fact, these experiences have given us the equivalent of 1000 years of wisdom—a statement that is no exaggeration.

There have been interviews on 500 more topics across various television programs. Such an extensive experience in a single lifetime is rare. I often reminisce about everyone who made this possible. Some of these achievers are no longer with us, but I still feel their presence as if they continue to talk to me in my dreams. What a blessing, isn't it?

Personality Development Training

Thousands of training programs have helped introduce various dimensions of personality development and provide guidance to many individuals. Some participants experience noticeable transformation on the very day of the training itself.

This has been a deeply fulfilling experience, making me a millionaire in terms of satisfaction. It gives me immense pride to be recognized as a trainer and mentor.

A Poem on the Mirror

During one of our personality development training sessions, our student and artist, Ravinath Pattanashetty, wrote this poem.

The Mirror

How many faces does the mirror have?
It simply reflects us, asking for no favor.

An old man, a young girl,
A thief, a lame person, the rich, the poor—
It shows each one their true self.

Filling colors in a child's dreams,
Weeping when we cry, smiling when we laugh,
Creating illusions and nurturing desires.

Even when shattered into pieces,
It still speaks only the truth,
For it knows nothing but honesty.

Keeping nothing for itself,
Losing nothing of its own,
It sees everything with clarity.

Selfless, colorless,
A mirror that we love,
A mirror with countless faces, countless reflections.

Jayaprakash Nagathihalli YouTube Channel & Transformation Unlimited Youtube Channel

For the past six years, we have been posting one to two videos almost every day, making this a powerful platform for our thoughts.

Our online student discussions, achiever interviews, and new ideas continue to emerge consistently. Many YouTube Live sessions, along with Q&A programs, have provided a unique experience.

The 'Mirror Beauty' Sculpture

The *Mirror Beauty* sculptures at Belur's ancient temple are remarkable. They remind us of the importance of self-reflection and continuous refinement. These intricate carvings also represent the essence of true craftsmanship.

2.

Personality Development – A Ladder to Life

Personality

When describing someone's appearance, we might say they are six feet tall, have an average build, wheatish complexion, a smiling face, curly hair, a dignified walk, a straight nose, and shining eyes. However, this is only the external appearance of a person and not their complete personality. This outward look is merely a part of their overall personality.

A person's nature, mindset, behavior, way of responding to the world, speech, attire, skills, knowledge, emotions, ambitions, and life goals together form a holistic picture of what we call "personality."

Each person has a unique way of speaking, expressions, behavior, smile, and reactions to situations, which set them apart from others.

Personality is shaped by a variety of factors, including inborn nature, upbringing, family environment, society, traditions, education, friends, teachers, beliefs, values, skills, financial situation, age, and health.

Education teaches us the two fundamental aspects of life:

1. What is life?
2. What is the world?

With this knowledge, we can lead a peaceful and fulfilling life.

One Life, One Body

From a general perspective, we all have only one life, and there is no guarantee that we will wake up tomorrow.

Making Life Meaningful

Life is a gift from God or nature, which we can experience only as long as the life force remains within us.

We all have just one body, so we must strive to live purposefully and meaningfully.

Challenges in Life

- Struggles for survival
- Overpopulation
- Unending violence
- Unemployment crisis
- Cruelty and inhumanity
- Self-centered politics
- Blind imitation of Western culture
- Environmental destruction

- Uncontrolled urbanization
- Confused youth
- Materialistic obsession
- Increasing complexities
- Cutthroat competition
- The dark side of civilization

The Key to Success

In today's technological age, where life is becoming more stressful, various spiritual leaders, psychologists, trainers, and mentors have shared the science of life, the art of living, and principles for a fulfilling life.

This is what we call Personality Development.

Elements of Personality Development

- Physical senses
- Intelligence & knowledge
- Emotions
- Social relationships
- Spiritual inclination

Achieving success in life, continuous growth, and harmonious relationships is what personality development is all about.

Why Are People Unhappy?

1. The first desire of every human is to survive at any cost.
2. Lack of basic necessities – food, clothing, and shelter.
3. Unrealistic desires and ambitions.
4. Excessive expectations from life and people.

5. Constant disappointments.
6. Suppressed grief or anger (leading to depression or anxiety).
7. Emotional distress – sadness, crying, suffering (with no one to comfort).
8. Broken families and relationships (without support).
9. Unexpected disasters or tragic events.

If we want to avoid these problems, we must change our approach to life, take responsibility, and embrace a new way of living.

Balancing the Three Factors

1. Family
2. Workplace
3. Society

   Balancing these three aspects of life is essential for holistic personality development.

Five Aspects of a Complete Personality

1. Moral Development
2. Intellectual Growth
3. Social Awareness
4. Emotional Maturity
5. Physical Well-being

We must recognize our inner potential, stay strong-minded, and climb one step at a time to reach our goals.

Achieving personal success is not enough—we must also help others succeed.

Three Pillars of Success

1. Attitude (Our mindset and approach to life)
2. Skills (Our abilities and expertise)
3. Knowledge (Our learning and wisdom)

Positive Personality Traits

- Strong determination
- High self-confidence
- Hard work
- Consistent efforts
- Belief in one's abilities
- Friendly nature
- Good communication skills
- Enthusiasm for life
- Readiness to adapt

All these together form a positive attitude.

Essential Life Skills

- Communication skills
- Time management
- Building relationships
- Problem-solving
- Teamwork and collaboration
- Leadership qualities
- Handling stress effectively
- Making the right decisions at the right time
- Persuasion and influence

These skills are crucial for success in life.

Knowledge

1. Expertise in our field
2. General knowledge
3. Practical business knowledge

Success is never easy—we must make conscious efforts to lead a peaceful and meaningful life.

By stepping out of our comfort zone, we can explore new opportunities and see life from a broader perspective.

With strong determination and teamwork, we can even create miracles.

There are no limits to intelligence, potential, or achievements.

Remember: With sheer willpower, even a dwarf (Vamana) can transform into a giant (Trivikrama).

True Beauty

True beauty is a combination of inner and outer personality.

Like the famous song from Kannada cinema says:

"Heaven and hell are right here—nowhere else!"

We must understand this truth and live a meaningful life.

What to Avoid?

✗ Ego
✗ Anger
✗ Stress
✗ Anxiety
✗ Depression

What to Embrace?

✓ Self-confidence
✓ Patience
✓ Selflessness
✓ Happiness
✓ Active participation in life
✓ Living in the present
✓ Focused attention

A Beautiful Life

"Life should be as sweet as words, as light as a flower, and as sweet tempered as a cow."

— D.V. Gundappa (DVG)

By cultivating a positive mindset, acquiring essential skills, and continuously learning, we can achieve both personal and professional success.

Let's embrace personality development and make life extraordinary! ✦

2A.

Personality Development

Sadhana Kayakini, TVN Murthy, and Mohammad Anwar

Jayaprakash: Viewers, a warm welcome to our program. You often hear the term "personality development." Sometimes, we feel that personality development is something that happens only to others, not to us. We also hear about numerous training programs on personality development. It is a continuous process that extends from childhood to old age. Today, let's understand the relevance and necessary methods of personality development.

We have three experts with us today, each of whom has conducted hundreds of training sessions on human resource development. First, let me introduce Sadhana Kayakini. She is the president of *Buoyancy*, an organization dedicated entirely to training. She has designed special training programs for children, youth, women, and companies. She has also been honored with awards from *Rotary* and *Junior Chamber.*

Next, we have TVN Murthy from Tumkur. Although he studied automobile engineering, he is now a businessman. He has earned the *Excel* title from *Junior Chamber International* and has served as a national-level office bearer in the organization. During his tenure as a *Zonal President*, he introduced three audio cassettes—*Maatu Mallige, Nade Nudi,* and *Sukhi Dampatya Jeevana*—on various subjects. He is also deeply concerned about wildlife and environmental conservation.

Finally, we have Mohammad Anwar from Haveri. He is an *Assistant Controller* in the *Weights and Measures Department.* He is a member of *Junior Chamber Kundapura* and an internationally certified trainer under *Junior Chamber International.* He has conducted numerous training programs at the international level.

Viewers, many people think of *personality development* as increasing their weight by a few extra kilograms! But first, let's clarify what personality development actually means.

Jayaprakash: Sadhana, what does personality development mean from your perspective?

Sadhana Kaykini: We are all born as individuals, but if we receive encouragement from our families or attend training programs, the good qualities within us can emerge. Everyone possesses strengths and talents, but recognizing and refining them is what I consider personality development.

Jayaprakash: Murthy, what are your thoughts?

TVN Murthy: *Mohandas Karamchand Gandhi* was born as just an ordinary person, but he became *Mahatma Gandhi. Mother Teresa* was just an ordinary woman, but she became a world-renowned humanitarian. People began recognizing and respecting them because of their extraordinary personality traits. If *Gandhi* had remained an ordinary person, he would have simply been called *Gandhi*, not *Mahatma*. Similarly, *Mother Teresa* would not have been revered as she is today. This transformation happened due to their developed personalities.

In today's world, to truly succeed, one must stand out and be extraordinary. Otherwise, they will simply be left behind.

Jayaprakash: Right, Murthy! That reminds me of a saying: *"If you add 'extra' to 'ordinary,' you get 'extraordinary.'"* Identifying that 'extra' is the essence of personality development.

TVN Murthy: Exactly!

Jayaprakash: Anwar, what are your thoughts?

Mohammad Anwar: There is a saying that no human being in this world is insignificant. Every individual has greatness and uniqueness within them. However, they need to recognize and nurture it. Personality development is the process of identifying and utilizing one's strengths, talents, and unique qualities effectively. It is an essential process for everyone.

Jayaprakash: Murthy, personality development does not happen automatically. Then why are training programs necessary?

TVN Murthy: Personality development programs don't create something extraordinary out of nowhere. Instead, they help individuals recognize and refine qualities they already possess. These programs collect and present real-life experiences, allowing participants to understand and apply them. The purpose is to make individuals aware of their inherent abilities and help and utilize them effectively.

Jayaprakash: Some people wonder whether personality development is needed only for children, youth, or older adults. Who needs it the most?

Sadhana Kaykini: In the past, elders at home would guide their children and grandchildren, sharing life experiences and encouraging them. That, in itself, was personality development.

Jayaprakash: So it was naturally happening within families?

Sadhana: Yes! But nowadays, even if elders are present at home, we don't have time to sit with them and listen to their experiences. That is why personality development programs are necessary for everyone. However, if we focus on children and women, they can bring positive change to their families as well.

Jayaprakash: You seem particularly concerned about women's development.

Sadhana: Yes! Housewives often feel a lack of confidence compared to working women. They may think, *"I am just staying at home; what am I really accomplishing?"* This can lead to self-doubt. If we provide them with personality development training, they can become more confident and happier.

Jayaprakash: Murthy, what do you think?

TVN Murthy: As you mentioned earlier, personality development is needed from childhood until death. *Life is a process of learning.* Every day, we learn something new.

Why is personality development particularly crucial for young people? In school, we learn physics, mathematics, science, languages, etc., but we don't learn *how to live life effectively*. That is why personality development workshops and real-life experiences are necessary.

Many people say that today's youth lack respect for elders and teachers, or that they are easily frustrated. However, if you observe, even young people get emotional during movie scenes. This shows that deep down, they do have emotions and values. However, today's society and environment often suppress them.

Due to this, young people struggle to express their potential and emotions properly. Therefore, creating an environment where they can recognize and develop their personality is crucial.

Jayaprakash: You say that this is especially necessary for young people?

TVN Murthy: Definitely.

Jayaprakash: The government has also recognized this and, in a recent budget speech, the Chief Minister prioritized conducting more personality development programs under the Youth Services and Sports Department.

TVN Murthy: Yes. That's because it is a transformational age. When we are young, we undergo immense changes. Perhaps, what I learn at this age, I will understand better in my old age. The experiences we gain today become the real-life lessons that stay with us forever. So, personality development is extremely important for young people. They must learn about it.

Jayaprakash: Now, many young people have crossed that phase and entered old age.

TVN Murthy: Certainly.

Jayaprakash: But don't they also need personality development?

Anwar: As Ms. Sadhana said, personality development starts from home. Whether it is for young people or children, from a certain age perspective, we cannot say that personality development stops once a person reaches a certain stage. We have all heard about Plato's example. Even on his deathbed, he was eager to learn more. Similarly, when Sir M. Visvesvaraya was asked what he needed, he reportedly said, "Bring me a dictionary," as he still wanted to keep learning.

Our parents, though they may not have had formal training, guided us on how to grow and succeed in life. They did not have formal training boards, but they taught us the art of living. Sending us to school was a decision they made based on their life experiences. Similarly, personality development is necessary for older people as well. The need for training has now been streamlined, and we have labeled it as personality development.

Even today, if you visit some offices, you will find many employees who have grown professionally but have not developed the right mindset. They may have degrees and qualifications, but if they do not upgrade their skills and thinking in this modern technological world, continuous learning becomes essential. Personality development helps in this process by ensuring that people stay updated and adopt to the changes.

Jayaprakash: Because when people move from youth to old age, many of them find it difficult to accept and adopt to this transition.

TVN Murthy: Yes, mentally...

Jayaprakash: Mentally, they also need to be prepared. For example, when some people retire, they feel like life is over. In that sense, what Anwar said is very important.

TVN Murthy: Many people are not mentally prepared for old age. When they were young, they never thought about how they would behave when they got older. But as Anwar mentioned, what elderly people say at that stage often becomes final for others—it becomes like a rule. At home, they act as judges, making decisions that affect the whole family. If they are not updated and educated about the present-day world, their rulings could have a negative impact. That is also a part of personality development.

Anwar: Exactly, Mr. Murthy. The reason elderly people's words hold such weight is because of their vast life experience.

Jayaprakash: That wealth of experience...

Anwar: Based on that, we have a subject in our training programs called "Practical Analysis," where we divide human psychology into three compartments—how a child's mind works, how a young person's mind works, and how an elderly person's mind works. This doesn't mean that you need to be a child to have a childlike mind, or that you need to be old to think like an elder. The key is to maintain a balanced mindset at all stages of life.

For example, when watching a movie with family, if an older person sits there being too serious, it takes away from the joy of the moment. Similarly, when in nature, one should be able to enjoy and appreciate the beauty with a childlike sense of wonder.

Jayaprakash: Okay. Now, we need to discuss the topics covered in personality development programs. Let's introduce those subjects to our viewers.

Sadhana: One major issue is hesitation. If you hesitate, personality development becomes impossible. People often think, "Oh no, what if someone is watching me? What if they laugh at me?" If such hesitation exists, personality development is not possible. To overcome this, we focus on public speaking. Speaking in front of a crowd builds confidence, helping people gradually overcome their hesitation.

Jayaprakash: Public speaking?

Sadhana: Yes, public speaking. That is our main focus.

Jayaprakash: So, they become good speakers.

Sadhana Kaikini: Yes.

Jayaprakash Nagathihalli: And through that, they build self-confidence. Mr. Murthy, what do you say?

TVN Murthy: J.P., personality development topics keep evolving over time. If I am teaching the same training program today that I conducted years ago, it may no longer be relevant. Society keeps changing, and we must update our training accordingly.

For example, recently, we have been discussing human relationships a lot. I run a blood bank in my hometown with a group of young volunteers. One day, I received a phone call from someone urgently needing O-positive blood. It was a life-or-death situation, and they needed the blood within three hours. I asked, "What is your blood group?" He replied, "O-positive."

So, I asked, "If you are the son, why don't you donate your own blood?" He said, "Why should I give my blood for free?" This response shocked me. It's not that he was unwilling to help his father, but rather that the sense of relationships and responsibilities had diminished in our society.

How we behave with our spouses, parents, children, teachers, neighbors, and colleagues is crucial. Today, people get angry over minor issues and cut ties over small misunderstandings. This is why training in human relationships is essential.

Another important topic is that today's world values talented people, not just educated ones. A person with an M.A. degree who doesn't know the price of a postcard is of little use in the real world. It's not just about book knowledge but also practical knowledge—the art of living.

Self-confidence is another essential aspect. Many people feel hesitant when they have to meet an official or talk to a new person. We need to build confidence so that they can face any situation without fear.

Additionally, positive thinking is crucial. People often have a negative mindset, fearing failure or avoiding risks. But success doesn't come overnight. In today's world, many people seek shortcuts—investing money expecting double returns in no time. However, patience is key.

If we always think negatively, we would cry at every birthday because it means another year has passed. Instead, we should celebrate with a positive outlook, thinking about the opportunities ahead.

There are countless such topics in personality development that are necessary for today's world.

Jayaprakash: Mr. Murthy, how do you measure success?

TVN Murthy: J.P., success is measured by the end result—whether you achieved what you wanted and to what extent.

For example, if I receive 100 rupees or get a job, that may be a success for me. But success differs for each person based on their desires and goals.

Imagine you are hungry, and someone gives you a piece of cake. That cake is a success for you at that moment. But for someone who just ate lunch, the same cake may seem unnecessary.

So, success is defined by individual needs and the opportunities available.

Anwar: Yes. Now, as Mr. Murthy mentioned, Jayaprakash sir, when I joined the Junior Chamber movement, I realized that training is a system through which individuals can be developed by providing training. However, when I joined the Junior Chamber, as Sadhana mentioned, we only found limited topics such as speech skills, human relations, and business analysis.

As we participated in these training sessions and developed ourselves as trainers, we questioned why we should limit ourselves to only these topics. Instead, we should focus on what is relevant to people today and provide training accordingly.

For example, as Mr. Murthy mentioned, people today expect fast returns. Whatever they invest—whether knowledge, effort, or money—they want immediate results. For instance, when I travel with children, I ask them, "Have you seen a ragi (finger millet) plant?" I ask them how it looks. It saddens me that they do not know. This made me think that perhaps children need to be taken to see these plants and understand what ragi and jowar (sorghum) are.

Similarly, today, some animals can only be seen in zoos. As trainers, we take all these factors into account and design our training topics accordingly. We identify the needs of different groups and create training sessions that are relevant to them.

Jayaprakash: Now that you say you design training programs, how do you incorporate different methodologies? What are the different methods you use in training?

TVN Murthy: There are various ways to teach.

Jayaprakash: Sadhana, what do you think?

Sadhana: Self-confidence is the first and most common requirement. As Anwar mentioned, we ask trainees about their instructional objectives. When we assess their needs, we find that many young people need training in facing interviews. Similarly, for women, we can offer guidance on improving their family and social life.

Jayaprakash: Do you conduct mock interviews as part of the training?

Sadhana: Yes, absolutely. We conduct mock interviews, provide questionnaires, and help participants reflect on their strengths and weaknesses. Their self-confidence is shaped by this process. We tailor our methodologies based on different groups.

Jayaprakash: Do you use a scoring system to evaluate participants and suggest areas for improvement?

Sadhana: Yes, we do. Based on the scores, we determine what kind of training is necessary.

Jayaprakash: So, you assess and judge their needs.

Sadhana: Exactly, we evaluate and guide them accordingly.

Anwar: When it comes to training, as you mentioned, we, as trainers, do not sell products in a market. We offer training on various subjects, and those who are interested can take advantage of it.

Sadhana: That's right.

Anwar: There are numerous local organizations, youth groups, and women's associations. They can discuss their training needs in meetings and request programs that will help their members succeed in life.

Jayaprakash: So, you're saying that training must be customized based on the time, place, and people involved?

Anwar: Yes, it has to be adapted accordingly.

Jayaprakash: That means the training methods also change accordingly. Let's talk about those methods.

TVN Murthy: Training methods vary. If I were to speak for three hours straight, people wouldn't be able to sit and listen. Nobody wants to keep looking at my face for that long!

Anwar: That's true.

TVN Murthy: Training needs variety. It is a science. Trainers must continuously research what interests people and what doesn't. If we plan a training session for three hours, three days, or even 15 days, we must ensure people can stay engaged.

The first method is oral instruction—lecturing.

Jayaprakash: Public speaking.

TVN Murthy: Yes, speaking or giving a lecture.

Mohammed Anwar: A seminar.

TVN Murthy: Yes, a seminar is another technique. The second method is learning through games. We conduct activities where participants learn something through the outcome of a game.

Jayaprakash: The message from the game.

TVN Murthy: Yes, the entire message of the game is a learning experience. Training can also be done through television programs.

Anwar: For example, cooking shows.

TVN Murthy: Yes, cooking shows are a form of training.

Anwar: Television is a very effective medium. Housewives, who may not attend training sessions, can still learn through TV programs while managing household chores.

TVN Murthy: Not just that, but music can also be a technique. Singing brings out hidden talents in people. It builds confidence.

Another method is practical demonstrations. Some people might think they can't do something, but when given hands-on experience, they realize how easy it is. This practical approach helps boost confidence.

We also use questionnaires to assess skills and abilities. Additionally, we provide audio materials, such as cassette tapes, which people can listen to while commuting.

There are many different training methods, and we adopt them as needed.

Jayaprakash: That was a great explanation of training methods. Now, in the 21st century, where we focus on the well-being of society, what message do you have for the audience?

Sadhana: Everyone has good qualities. God has given each of us something special. We must do something meaningful in life.

Jayaprakash: Each person has unique strengths.

Sadhana: Exactly! We must discover and use them to make our lives meaningful. That's my advice.

Jayaprakash: Murthy sir, your thoughts?

TVN Murthy: We are all born champions. The fact that we were born as humans among so many species itself is a great success. From the moment we were born, we have been overcoming challenges. Sometimes, we may fear small obstacles. But through personality development training, people become better individuals. When people become better, society improves. When society improves, we can build a great nation—an integrated and prosperous India.

Jayaprakash: Anwar?

Anwar: As Murthy said, opportunities do not come only to the educated. Success does not belong only to scholars. Those with determination and a strong will can achieve anything.

We should not limit personality development to a specific group. Whether for children, youth, or any other section of society, personality development training should be provided to everyone.

Jayaprakash: So, in your view, training is necessary for all sections of society.

Anwar: Yes, training should be offered at every stage and to every group in different ways. This will help people succeed in today's competitive world.

Jayaprakash: In this competitive era, personality development is essential for everyone. Listening to the expert opinions shared today makes this very clear. We all need self-confidence.

On behalf of everyone, I thank Sadhana, TVN Murthy, and Mohammed Anwar for sharing their insights. Your discussion was truly enlightening.

I also extend my thanks to our audience. Thank you all.

3.

The Mental Mirror

Beautiful Mind, Beautiful Personality

A person's mental personality depends on their internal state of mind, emotions, and thoughts. It reflects how their external behavior, decisions, and relationships are shaped.

Mental personality is influenced by several factors:

1. Self-Confidence – A person's belief in themselves and their abilities.

2. Decision-Making – The ability to analyze problems and make quick, effective decisions.
3. Emotional Strength – Managing emotions and responding appropriately to challenges.
4. Self-Reflection – Evaluating one's behavior and decisions to strive for self-improvement.
5. Problem-Solving – The ability to remain calm under stress and tackle challenges effectively.

For a mentally healthy personality, self-control, courage, and commitment are essential.

Wisdom from Great Thinkers on the Power of the Mind

Many eminent personalities have emphasized the role of the mind in achieving success:

1. Mahatma Gandhi – *"A man is but the product of his thoughts; what he thinks, he becomes."*
2. Abraham Lincoln – *"People are as happy as they decide to be."*
3. Swami Vivekananda – *"You are what you think. All that you are arises from your thoughts."*
4. Buddha – *"Your thoughts shape your life."*
5. Eleanor Roosevelt – *"No one can make you feel inferior without your consent."*
6. Steve Martin – *"The conscious mind is the editor, the subconscious mind is the writer."*
7. Thomas Edison – *"Never go to sleep without giving your subconscious a task."*
8. W. Clement Stone – *"You influence your subconscious mind through verbal repetition."*

These quotes highlight the importance of the mind and its power in shaping our lives.

Understanding the Mind

Understanding the mind involves analyzing our thoughts, emotions, and behaviors while engaging in self-reflection. Some ways to achieve this include:

1. Self-Reflection – Analyzing daily thoughts, behaviors, and decisions.
2. Meditation – Calming the mind, gaining clarity, and harnessing inner strength.
3. Emotional Awareness – Understanding why emotions arise and how we respond to them.
4. Journaling – Expressing thoughts and emotions through writing.
5. Cognitive Awareness – Evaluating whether our thoughts and decisions are rational and beneficial.
6. Communication – Sharing thoughts and emotions with others to gain insights.
7. Spiritual Study – Exploring philosophy, spirituality, and self-improvement literature.

Different Aspects of the Mind

The mind functions in multiple ways, which are categorized in psychology and philosophy:

1. Conscious Mind – The immediate awareness and thoughts we actively process.
2. Subconscious Mind – The storage of past experiences, habits, and emotions.

3. Unconscious Mind – Deep-seated emotions and thoughts that influence behavior unknowingly.
4. Active Mind – The mind's ability to respond to tasks and make quick decisions.
5. Creative Mind – Imagination and innovation that drive art, literature, and new ideas.
6. Professional Mind – The thought processes involved in career decisions and work strategies.
7. Social Mind – The way we interact with others and build relationships.

These aspects collectively shape how a person thinks, reacts, and makes decisions.

The Mind in Poetry

Many poets and writers have explored the vastness of the mind:

1. Kuvempu – "Wherever the body may be, the mind keeps wandering; It soars beyond limits, embracing the unseen."
2. DVG – "The mind has no boundaries; it flies higher than the sky, floating beyond reach."
3. Unknown Poet – "The power of the mind should never be forgotten; it shapes reality through persistent thought."
4. K.S. Nissar Ahmed – "The depth of the mind knows no bounds; it soars through time, seeking answers beyond reach."
5. M. Govinda Pai – "The external mind craves the world, while the inner mind remains at peace; One is filled with desires, the other with fulfillment."

These poems illustrate the complex and profound nature of the mind.

The Mind as a Tool for Growth

The mind plays a crucial role in personal, professional, and spiritual growth. Here's how:

1. Positive Thinking – A positive mindset builds confidenceaa and resilience.
   Example: Believing "I can do it" drives success.
2. Creativity & Innovation – The mind inspires fresh ideas and solutions.
   Example: Finding innovative ways to solve problems.
3. Self-Awareness – Understanding strengths and weaknesses leads to clarity in life goals.
4. Growth Mindset – A learning-oriented mindset enables continuous improvement.
   Example: Viewing challenges as opportunities to grow.
5. Problem-Solving Ability – A calm mind can tackle challenges with strategic thinking.
6. Emotional Control & Peace – Managing emotions helps in decision-making during tough times.
7. Self-Confidence & Courage – A strong mind faces challenges fearlessly.
   Example: Overcoming fear of failure through mental strength.
8. Meditation & Inner Peace – Mindfulness enhances focus and clarity.
9. Character Development – Strong values lead to success in personal and social life.aa

Mind Over Matter

The mind is the driving force, and the body is the vehicle. To reach any destination, both must function optimally.

- "Where there is a mind, there is a way; Where there is a goal, there is success."
- "Don't just react, respond."
- "A pure mind leads to a healthy life."

When the mind is disciplined and empowered, it brings success in every aspect of life.

Conclusion

The power of the mind shapes our reality. Training the mind with positive thoughts, self-awareness, and mental discipline leads to greater success, happiness, and inner peace.

"If you master your mind, you master your life."

— Jayaprakash Nagathihalli

3A.

A Discussion on the Conscious Mind in an Online Class

This conversation is a discussion from an online class about the conscious mind , led by Jayaprakash Nagathihalli and involving multiple participants. Here's a translation of the key points:

Jayaprakash: Today's topic is the conscious mind, which refers to being in the present moment. Whatever we are at this moment, that is our conscious mind.

Manasa: Right now, we are talking about the conscious mind and are actively participating in this meeting, meaning we are in a conscious mindset. The main aspect we need to learn in this state is communication—how we should speak consciously, behave, and express ideas effectively.

When we talk about consciousness, it also applies to physical appearance—a well-dressed person with a good presentation is considered well-prepared. But along with that, communication skills should also be well-developed. I would like to hear from Ravi Sir about what he thinks of the conscious mind.

Ravi: Today, we are discussing a very important topic—the conscious mind. In simple terms, awareness of our internal and external existence is what defines the conscious mind.

There are four key aspects of the conscious mind:

1. **Thinking**
2. **Feeling**
3. **Sensing**
4. **Intuiting**

The conscious mind is extremely important because our physical actions, achievements, and future goals all depend on it. There is a saying:

"What we are today is the result of our thoughts from yesterday, and what we think today builds our tomorrow."

This means that our future is shaped by our present thoughts.

I'd like to share a story:

A man was sitting under a tree. Near him, there were two holes in the ground.

- From one hole, a snake came out and bit him, causing him pain and injury.
- From the second hole, a mouse emerged. When the man saw it, he angrily hit the mouse, even though it had done nothing wrong.
- Later, the mouse bit him in retaliation, and he screamed in pain.
- When he saw another snake coming from the first hole, he panicked and suffered a heart attack.

Now, the question is: What caused his death? The snake or the mouse?

The answer is: his own mind.

This teaches us that instead of negative thinking, we should cultivate positive and necessary creative thinking.

"No poison can kill a positive thinker. No medicine can cure a negative thinker."

That is the power of the conscious mind.

Manasa: To work consciously, we need experience, expertise, and self-confidence. Many people have experience and skills, but without confidence, their consciousness gets disturbed in critical situations. Let's hear from Pratibha Ma'am about her experience.

Pratibha: The conscious mind plays a key role in decision-making, planning, communication, and skill organization.

- Activities like brushing our teeth or taking a bath are not part of the conscious mind—they are part of the subconscious mind because they happen out of habit.
- But when we have to speak in a meeting or give a speech, we cannot just say anything that comes to mind—we need preparation and conscious thinking.
- Similarly, when we drive a car, we must consciously control the steering, deciding when to turn left or right. That is why a conscious mind is essential for safety and success.

Jayaprakash: Now, let's hear from Narayanaswamy Sir about his thoughts on the conscious mind.

Narayanaswamy: We must be conscious and aware in our work and decision-making. However, overthinking can sometimes lead to confusion. There is a saying:

"Even nectar can turn into poison if consumed in excess."

If we are too conscious, we might start overanalyzing everything and get stuck in indecision. So, while consciousness is important, we must also maintain a balance.

Jayaprakash: Narayanaswamy Sir made an interesting point about not being overly conscious. But at the same time, we must always be alert and aware in life.

Being conscious means living in the present. If we are not conscious, our subconscious mind remains inactive, making us like Kumbhakarna (a mythological figure known for his deep sleep).

While the subconscious mind controls 80% of our actions, it is only through the conscious mind that we can access and influence it. This is why understanding the mind is so important.

Even leading scientific institutions like the Indian Institute of Science have been conducting extensive research on the brain and mind. The conscious mind, when trained properly, leads to better decision-making, success, and awareness in life.

Conclusion

This discussion emphasized the importance of the conscious mind in everyday life, decision-making, and personal growth. The key takeaways are:

- Stay in the present moment and be aware of your thoughts and actions.
- Balance your consciousness—don't overthink or be too rigid.
- Positive thinking is powerful—it can shape your future and well-being.
- Conscious actions lead to success, whether in communication, decision-making, or daily tasks.

3B.

The Power of the Subconscious Mind

Subconscious Mind

Many thoughts arise in our minds. As Gautama Buddha said:

- What you think, you become.
- What you feel, you attract.
- What you imagine, you create.

The first thing a human must discover is the power of the mind. It is deeper than the ocean and vaster than the sky. This mental strength can only be attained through awareness, and once achieved, you can control an immense force.

By understanding this, we can distance ourselves from unnecessary mental stress. There is substantial evidence that the subconscious mind serves as a bridge between our conscious mind and unlimited knowledge. The subconscious mind enhances attention, focus, flexibility, memory, speed, and creativity.

- Conscious Mind = The awake mind
- Subconscious Mind = The latent mind

Quotes on the Power of the Subconscious Mind

"Achievement comes out of firing our subconscious mind with the belief that 'I will win'."

– A.P.J. Abdul Kalam

"There is only one process of healing, and that is FAITH. There is only one healing power, namely, your subconscious mind."

– Joseph Murphy

Having faith is essential. If we have faith, the subconscious mind contains healing power.

"You can go as far as your mind lets you. What you believe, remember, you can achieve."

Your mind can take you as far as you allow it. The subconscious mind plays a significant role in our success and achievements in life.

"Your subconscious mind does not know the difference between an actual experience that produces an emotion and an emotion that you fabricate by thought alone."

– Dr. Joe Dispenza

The subconscious mind accepts whatever you feed it. "You reap what you sow." If you tell your subconscious mind, *"I am foolish,"* it will believe you. If you tell it, *"I am intelligent,"* it will accept that too. Hence, we must be careful about what we feed our minds. Our thought process must always be positive.

Albert Einstein is said to have effectively utilized the power of the subconscious mind. Many people worldwide have undergone miraculous transformations due to their knowledge application and strong self-confidence. You too can achieve positive changes in your life by harnessing the power of your mind. This process is based on your thought waves, daily activities, mindset, and goals.

Ultimately, this results in unlimited happiness. We must ask ourselves various questions. Asking questions brings clarity.

Thought-Provoking Questions

1. Why is one person unhappy while another is joyful?
2. Why does one person achieve wealth and success while another struggles in poverty?
3. Why does one person gain recognition and fame, while another remains unnoticed?
4. Why does one person progress rapidly in their career while another remains stagnant despite years of hard work?
5. Why does one person maintain good health despite hardships, while another suffers from illness despite minor health issues?
6. Why do some people face continuous hardships even when they think positively?
7. Why do some people, despite their undisciplined and unhealthy lifestyle, remain strong, while others who

follow a disciplined life suffer from physical and mental health issues?

8. Why do some people find happiness and peace in marriage, while others feel trapped and distressed?

Think honestly. Do you have answers to these questions? Asking the right questions brings clarity.

The Subconscious Mind – The Treasure That Fulfills Your Desires

The subconscious mind is a treasure within you. You can unlock it by deeply understanding yourself.

The Oxford definition of the subconscious mind states that it is "the part of the mind of which one is not fully aware but which influences one's actions and feelings."

Many people are unaware of the subconscious mind, but it plays a significant role in shaping our actions and emotions.

Conscious vs. Subconscious Mind

Conscious Mind (10%)

- Willpower
- Logical Thinking
- Critical Thinking
- Long-term Memory

Subconscious Mind (90%)

- Beliefs
- Emotions

- Habits
- Values
- Protective Reactions
- Long-term Memory
- Imagination
- Intuition

"There is no greater entity than a human, and there is no greater organ in a human than the brain."

– William Hamilton

The subconscious mind is a field of consciousness. Every thought that enters the conscious mind through the five senses is categorized and recorded in this field. This thought can be recalled whenever needed. – Napoleon Hill

The subconscious mind works on its own, whether or not you try to influence it. It continuously processes information.

If you fail to plant the right aspirations in your subconscious mind, it will adopt whatever thoughts come its way. Due to negligence, it absorbs random thoughts and ideas.

The subconscious mind acts like a radio receiver or intermediary. It converts our prayers into a form that the infinite intelligence can understand. This infinite intelligence then provides an answer in the form of an idea or thought. To communicate with the subconscious mind, you must speak its language – the language of feelings and emotions.

Reprogramming the Subconscious Mind for Learning

Negative thoughts can be transformed into positive affirmations:

- I am dumb → I am intelligent
- I cannot pass → I will pass
- This subject is difficult → Every subject is simple
- I cannot remember things → I have excellent memory
- I have no concentration → I am focused
- Studying is boring → Studying is enjoyable

Achieving Goals Using the Subconscious Mind

- I have the ability to reach my goals.
- I focus my mind on achieving my goal.
- I write down my goal and review it daily.
- I ensure fear does not affect me.
- I remain honest.

Overcoming Bad Habits

You have the freedom to choose good or bad habits. Habits are controlled by the subconscious mind.

- The real reason people drink alcohol is negative and destructive thinking.
- Most people drink because they do not accept their true potential.

Overcoming Fears

- Fear of losing dignity
- Fear of death

- Fear of illness
- Fear of new places
- Fear of new people
- Fear of public speaking
- Fear of failure

Affirmations to Overcome Fear:

- *I will overcome this fear.*
- *I have already conquered this fear.*
- *I speak with balance and confidence.*

By understanding and utilizing the power of the subconscious mind, you can transform your life and achieve happiness, success, and well-being.

Social Relationships

Think about others the way you want them to think about you.

Believe about others the way you want them to believe about you.

Treat others the way you want to be treated.

Resolving Marital Problems Through the Subconscious Mind

Divorce begins in the mind.

- An irritable wife
- An absent-minded husband
- Doubt
- Ego

Solutions for Resolving Marital Issues

The ignorance of mental and spiritual laws is the root cause of all marital troubles.

- Love and Compatibility
- No Fear Towards Your Partner
- Mutual Prayer
- Mutual Appreciation

For Wealth

The subconscious mind is like a bank. It is an eternal financial institution. Whatever you deposit into it will grow. Whether it is thoughts of wealth or poverty, it will multiply.

Hatred and jealousy are obstacles to the flow of wealth. Be happy for others' prosperity.
The barrier to wealth exists in your mind.

For Success

Success means a fulfilling life. If you are peaceful, happy, and enjoying the work you love, you are successful.

Become an expert in your field and strive to learn more than necessary.

Constant visualization activates the miraculous powers of the subconscious mind.

Overcoming Problems

- Accept and acknowledge the problem.

- Surrender the problem to your subconscious mind. Only it knows the solution.
- Have deep faith that the problem is already solved.

Subconscious Mind for Fulfilling Desires

For Health

Find what brings you healing. Have faith that the correct guidance to your subconscious mind will heal both your body and mind.

- Pray for the healing of loved ones.
- Believing in illness, loss, or pain is ignorance. Instead, believe in complete health, prosperity, peace, wealth, and harmony with nature.

Ways to Transfer Thoughts from the Conscious to the Subconscious Mind:

1. Create your blueprint.
2. Pray sincerely.
3. Visualize through images.
4. Mental Movie Technique.
5. Logical Approach.
6. Commanding Method.
7. Sleep Technique.
8. Gratitude Technique.
9. Positive Affirmations.

If you are praying for something but fear that it won't happen, or if you doubt whether the infinite intelligence will act on your prayer, then your prayer will be in vain.

The subconscious mind does not distinguish between right and wrong, or good and bad.

What Should You Think About?

"Whatever is true, whatever is noble, whatever is right, whatever is pure, whatever is lovely, whatever is admirable—think about such things."

– St. Paul

Thoughts cannot always be controlled, but words can be controlled. These words influence the subconscious mind, which then takes control over them. – Jane Fonda

The Power of the Subconscious Mind in Research

"The greatest discovery of the 20th century is the power of the subconscious mind activated by belief."

– William James

"Whatever you repeatedly affirm and feel deeply will become reality."

– Earl Nightingale

The conscious mind operates in the present and past, but the subconscious mind transcends time.

"The subconscious mind is 30,000 times more powerful than the conscious mind."

– Zig Ziglar

"The subconscious mind does not understand humor, jokes, or lies. It cannot differentiate between reality and imagination.
Whatever you visualize repeatedly becomes your destiny."

– Robert Collier

"Whether you think you can or think you can't, you are right both ways."

– Henry Ford

"Nothing is impossible. The word itself says 'I am possible'!"

– Audrey Hepburn

"The conscious mind is like an editor, while the subconscious mind is the writer."

– Steve Martin

Be mindful of the words you speak, as they will eventually control you.

– Paramahansa Yogananda

Never go to sleep without giving instructions to your subconscious mind.

– Thomas Edison

"If you want to change your life, first change your mind."

– Lauren Goldstein

You influence your subconscious mind through verbal repetition.

– W. Clement Stone

"Until you make the unconscious conscious, it will control your life, and you will call it fate."

– Carl Jung

If you fail the first time, do not get discouraged. With continuous practice, you can influence the subconscious mind.

Whatever thought or action you repeatedly impress upon your subconscious mind will eventually take form in reality.

The subconscious mind controls all major functions of the body and has the ability to solve your problems.

Whatever the conscious mind deeply believes and accepts as true, the subconscious mind absorbs and executes.

Think positively, and positive things will happen. Think negatively, and negative things will happen. Your thoughts shape your reality.

Whatever you wholeheartedly accept and believe in will be stored in your subconscious mind and manifest in your life.

3C.

The Super Concious Mind: A Path to Your Growth

Jayaprakash Nagathihalli

Dear all,
Namaste. I am Jayaprakash Nagathihalli.

I often say, *"Mind your mind, and it will mind you."* No matter how much we talk about the human mind, it never seems to be enough. Just like the vast ocean, many people have spoken about the mind in different ways, and many more will continue to do so. However, if we can bring a fresh perspective, it will be even more interesting.

The transcendental mind, the conscious mind, is the one that stays with us when we are awake. When we are in a state of awareness, we are alert, and this is the role of the conscious mind. The subconscious mind, on the other hand, is very powerful, but its switch is in the hands of the conscious mind. If the conscious mind is inactive, the subconscious mind remains dormant, like Kumbhakarna in deep sleep. But when awakened, it exhibits tremendous power, just like Kumbhakarna when he is roused from his slumber.

Now, what exactly is the superconscious mind? In the past, some people predicted what would happen in 50, 100, or even 300 years, and many of those predictions have turned out to be true. But how is that possible? Some of these things cannot be explained logically, yet they hold truth.

For instance, if someone approaches you with an intention to harm you, and you instinctively sense danger and become alert, it means your superconscious mind is active. This level of awareness goes beyond ordinary observation—it allows you to perceive things intuitively. I often use the word intuition, which is closely related to the superconscious mind.

Let me share a personal experience. In February 2022, I found myself in a situation where I instinctively felt something was wrong. I decided to leave that place, and later, I realized it was the right decision. Sometimes, we find ourselves in negative environments, but instead of staying there, it's better to move towards a more positive space. That day, my body vibrated like a mobile phone, as if warning me—*Jayaprakash, be careful!* That awareness helped me.

This proves that the first step towards activating the superconscious mind is being alert and aware of our conscious and subconscious minds. Once we acknowledge the power of the mind, it starts to awaken. If we affirm—*I have a sharp memory. My mind is powerful in all three states (conscious, subconscious, and superconscious)*—we begin to strengthen our mental faculties. However, if we constantly doubt ourselves, we hinder our own growth.

A truly positive person cannot be harmed by negativity. Their aura is so powerful that it burns away negativity. I have witnessed this firsthand—people who try to harm genuinely positive individuals often end up facing their downfall within a few months.

Honnavara Ravi

Today's topic is truly fascinating—the transcendental mind. While we have often heard about the conscious and subconscious minds, discussions on the superconscious mind are rare. To understand this, one must first grasp the concepts of the conscious and subconscious minds.

For example, when I speak, I am aware of what I am saying—this is the conscious mind at work. However, while speaking, I may also have an underlying sense of fear or anxiety, which is stored in the subconscious mind. Many times, we unknowingly allow negativity to build up in our subconscious mind. This is why people say, *"A lie repeated a hundred times becomes the truth."*

The superconscious mind, however, operates at a much deeper level. It is not easy for an ordinary person to comprehend. In physics, energy is said to be neither created nor destroyed, and when one reaches a heightened state of awareness, everything appears interconnected. At this level, one does not see problems as problems anymore. Everything in existence—whether living or non-living—feels connected. This superconscious state enables experiences of divine love and blessings.

How can one achieve this state? Through meditation, prayer, and affirmations. These practices help align emotions with the superconscious mind.

Manasa Tumakuru

Superconscious mind, as described by Jayaprakash Sir and Ravi Sir, is a complete energy force within us. One does not need formal education to access it; it is always present within. It is not just knowledge gained in this lifetime or previous ones—it is an inbuilt protective force.

There are several ways to activate the superconscious mind—through yoga, meditation, and the activation of chakras. When one systematically works on activating their chakras, the superconscious mind starts functioning at its peak.

In simple terms, the superconscious mind is like a power station within the human body. While the conscious mind helps us see, hear, and speak, and the subconscious mind keeps bodily functions running, the superconscious mind works as a protection shield for our entire existence. To strengthen it, one must engage in daily meditation. This will enhance our energy levels and protective shield without us even realizing it.

Ravinath

In spirituality, we refer to certain occurrences as miracles. Deep within the subconscious mind, there exists a super sense, which can manifest as extraordinary mental powers. These experiences can transcend the ordinary realm, and sometimes, people can foresee events or gain insights into unknown matters.

This ability is present in everyone, but it depends on an individual's spiritual and mental strength. Unlocking this power is difficult and requires deep spiritual practice. Some people experience this unexpectedly and perceive it as a miracle.

Jyoti Patil (Sirsi)

I have heard about the superconscious mind before, mainly from great yogis and saints. Certain Aghoris (ascetic practitioners) are believed to possess not just a sixth sense, but even a seventh sense, which grants them deeper awareness.

Krishnamurthy (Shivamogga)

Every human mind has the potential to become a superconscious mind, but it requires consistent effort. Through dedicated yoga and meditation, one can achieve this higher state of awareness. However, this is extremely rare, as it demands deep spiritual discipline.

Individuals who attain this state develop an extraordinary capacity—they do not experience difficulties in the way an ordinary person does. They perceive obstacles as mere trivialities. For them, solving problems becomes effortless, as if they are simply brushing away a speck of dust. The superconscious mind is the ultimate level of awareness.

Netravati

The superconscious mind acts like an inner compass. Even before we consciously recognize a situation, it provides subtle warnings and guidance. It may be about a decision, an action, or a daily life scenario.

We must pay close attention to these signals. By observing and acknowledging these subtle cues, we can align ourselves better with our higher consciousness.

3D.

Open Mind vs. Closed Mind

By Jayaprakash Nagathihalli

Today's discussion is about having an open mind versus a closed mind. A closed mind is like a sealed bottle—no matter how much water you pour in, it won't come out unless the bottle is opened. Similarly, an open mind allows thoughts to flow freely, both in and out.

An open mind helps us evolve toward what Kuvempu described as the "Vishwamanava" (universal human being). It encourages broad thinking, helping us transition from a narrow mindset to a broader, more inclusive perspective.

If someone has a closed mind, even when they are exposed to new ideas, they do not absorb them. That's why open-mindedness plays a very crucial role in our lives. It helps us understand life better and use our intelligence effectively. Let's hear Ravi's thoughts on this matter.

Ravi

This is a very important and necessary discussion. A closed mind can be compared to a stagnant well, whereas an open mind is like a flowing river. Stagnant water becomes polluted and harmful, while flowing water remains fresh and useful.

A person with a closed mind lacks acceptance, making it difficult for them to grow. Their empathy and sympathy levels are low because they believe that only their way is correct. Such a rigid mindset can be harmful. Those who do not update themselves or fail to accept new realities can fall behind. A closed mind is dangerous because it resists change and growth.

Netravati

A person with an open mind always has a thirst for knowledge and curiosity to move forward. They think deeply and strive for success.

A closed-minded person, on the other hand, refuses to consider others' opinions. They prefer to stay in their comfort zone and avoid challenges. There's an old village proverb that says, *"If a harp plays in front of a blind man, he will never know its beauty."* Similarly, a closed-minded person doesn't recognize valuable insights, even when they are right in front of them.

Subbu

Having an open mind brings people together and helps society grow. It allows individuals to listen and communicate better.

In contrast, a closed-minded person only listens to themselves and dismisses others' opinions. There's a proverb: *"If a village is burning, what does the accountant's hair have to do with it?"* This reflects how some people remain indifferent to important matters, believing that their way is the only way.

Vani

The mind is often compared to a monkey—it jumps from one thought to another. Hence, we must train our minds to be strong, both mentally and emotionally. The world respects strength, not weakness.

Many people struggle with mental challenges, and professional guidance can help them cope better. Professor C.R. Chandrashekhar, who has contributed immensely to mental health awareness, is an example of someone making a real difference. Counseling and guidance play a significant role in education and parenting.

Shailaja

Our mind consists of awareness, perception, thoughts, and memories. Sharing our knowledge with an open heart spreads positivity and improves society.

When someone is criticized for doing great work, it is actually a form of recognition. A mentor once told me:

"For a true achiever, criticism is the first step toward success."

A successful person does not get discouraged by negative remarks. Instead, they move forward, just like an elephant walks undisturbed despite barking dogs. We must learn to accept feedback with an open mind and differentiate between constructive criticism and unnecessary negativity.

Akkamahadevi once wrote:

**"If you build a house on a hill, wild animals will come;
If you build it on the shore, the waves will hit it;
If you are born in this world, both praise and criticism
will follow."**

This reminds us to stay positive, ignore negativity, and focus on personal growth.

Ravinath Pattana Shetty

While open-mindedness is essential, absolute openness is not always practical. Life requires balance and wisdom.

Doctors advise us not to lie to them, yet sometimes, even speaking the truth can put us in difficult situations. Similarly, lawyers encourage honesty, but in certain cases, openness can be risky.

So, while open-mindedness is valuable, we should also exercise discretion and judgment in how and when to express ourselves. Not everything needs to be shared openly—some matters are best kept private or discussed in the right context.

Jyoti Patil (Lawyer)

An open mind means speaking and listening with an open heart. This helps people understand each other better and find solutions to problems more quickly.

On the other hand, a closed mind blocks communication and growth. A person with a closed mind hides their true feelings and keeps their problems to themselves, which can lead to long-term emotional distress.

For example, in counseling and legal cases, people who open up and discuss their issues honestly are more likely to find resolutions than those who stay silent. Open-mindedness is crucial for personal and social harmony.

Thippeswamy

For personal growth, a person needs both open-mindedness and a degree of caution.

Some people spread negativity. While it's good to be open-minded, it's also important to filter out unnecessary negativity. We must listen, analyze, and accept only what helps us grow.

Conclusion by Jayaprakash

Each participant has shared their unique perspective. Such discussions help refine our thoughts and bring clarity. From ambiguity to clarity, open-mindedness enables us to grow.

A closed mind resists change, whereas an open mind embraces new experiences. The key is to strike a balance, knowing when to stay open and when to be cautious.

What are your thoughts? Do you agree that an open mind is the way forward?

4.

Intellectual Mirror

Intellectual Personality

An intellectual personality refers to an individual's cognitive abilities, reasoning skills, and the expansion of knowledge. It includes problem-solving abilities, logical reasoning, the capacity to understand new concepts, and an interest in learning—all of which are essential traits.

An intellectual personality is more thought-provoking and encourages deep reasoning. It enhances one's problem-solving skills, the ability to make philosophical decisions, and overall intellectual development.

Key Factors for Developing an Intellectual Personality

Several aspects contribute to enriching a person's intellectual ability and knowledge:

1. Curiosity
2. Learning and Knowledge Acquisition
3. Critical Thinking and Analysis
4. Creativity
5. Deep Reflection

6. Problem-Solving Skills
7. Patience and Discipline

Ways to Develop and Cultivate an Intellectual Personality

1. Daily Reading
2. Critical Thinking and Analysis
3. Meditation
4. Discussions and Debates
5. Teaching and Learning Techniques
6. Problem-Solving Activities
7. Spiritual and Philosophical Thinking
8. Positive Attitude
9. Engagement in Creative Activities
10. Applying What You Learn

Famous Intellectuals Who Exemplify Intellectual Personality

Many great thinkers and achievers have become renowned through their intellectual curiosity, innovation, and creativity. Some notable examples include:

1. **Albert Einstein** – A legendary physicist known for his profound theoretical insights and analytical skills. His *Theory of Relativity* stands as a testament to intellectual brilliance.
2. **Mahatma Gandhi** – A leader of India's independence movement and a philosophical thinker, Gandhi emphasized deep introspection and moral reasoning to promote social justice.
3. **Ernest Hemingway** – A renowned writer and artist, he expressed profound human experiences through his creative and intellectual writing.

4. **Martin Luther King Jr.** – A key figure in the civil rights movement, his powerful ideas and speeches helped shape the course of social justice through intellectual discourse.
5. **Maya Angelou** – A celebrated poet and writer, she conveyed deep societal messages through her literature and life teachings.
6. **Malala Yousafzai** – Through her advocacy for education, she demonstrated how learning and intellectual thought can transform society. Her courage and reflections are examples of intellectual excellence.

Inspirational Quotes on Intellectual Growth

1. **Albert Einstein:** "Education is what remains after one has forgotten what one has learned in school."
2. **Socrates:** "I know that I know nothing."
3. **Karl Marx:** "The philosophers have only interpreted the world, in various ways. The point, however, is to change it."
4. **Maya Angelou:** "When you know better, you do better."
5. **Mark Twain**: "A person who won't read has no advantage over one who can't read."
6. **Aristotle:** "We are what we repeatedly do. Excellence, then, is not an act, but a habit."

Essential Traits of Great Thinkers

To be recognized as a great thinker, one must cultivate certain intellectual traits. These qualities encourage deep reasoning and a strong presence in intellectual discourse:

1. Critical Thinking – The ability to analyze problems deeply and evaluate different perspectives.

2. Curiosity – A continuous eagerness to explore and learn new things.
3. Questioning and Reasoning – The habit of questioning existing beliefs and seeking deeper understanding.
4. Creativity – The ability to generate innovative ideas and solutions.
5. Self-Expression – The capability to articulate thoughts and share insights effectively.
6. Learning from Experience – Gaining wisdom by reflecting on past experiences.
7. Philosophical Perspective – Deep contemplation on life, society, and the universe.
8. Empathy – Understanding and considering the emotions and perspectives of others.
9. Commitment to Truth – Staying dedicated to intellectual pursuits and ethical reasoning.

These traits help individuals evolve into great thinkers and expand their intellectual capacities. By embracing a problem-solving mindset, making informed decisions, and engaging in creative activities, one can cultivate a truly intellectual personality.

4A.

Problem Solving

Jayaprakash Nagathihalli:

Dear friends, Namaskara!

I am Jayaprakash Nagathihalli. A warm welcome to the Jayaprakash Nagathihalli YouTube channel. In this video, we are going to discuss problem-solving—something that is essential for everyone, right? What do you say? This topic is undoubtedly relevant to all of you. So, make sure you watch the entire video and leave a comment. If you haven't subscribed to the Jayaprakash Nagathihalli YouTube channel yet, do it now. Like the video and share it with four to five people. That would be a gift from you to us. If you want to participate in an online class, just call 9341259267 and enquire about the next master class. OK?

Now, let's get into the topic—Problem Solving.

We all lead our lives in our unique ways, don't we? "Problem-solving" means understanding the problem and finding a solution, correct? If we want to move forward in life, we need to tackle problems, right? We constantly question ourselves: Is this right? Is this wrong? Is this how things should be? Do I know the answer?

One of the best ways to solve problems is using the Five W's and One H—When, Why, What, Where, Who, and How. Asking the right questions and organizing our thoughts helps us develop ideas. If we approach challenges with the mindset that every problem has a solution, we will always find a way forward.

However, in today's digital world, many people have trapped themselves in social media. But if we use these platforms wisely, they can help us grow. Opportunities are always available for those who seek them.

"When you focus on problems, you will have more problems. When you focus on possibilities, you will have more opportunities."

Isn't that beautiful? If you keep thinking only about problems, you will attract more problems. But if you focus on possibilities, new opportunities will open up for you. This quote makes it very clear.

"Sometimes, problems don't require a solution; they require a shift in perspective."

Every time we face a challenge, it tests our ability to handle it maturely.

"Life is not about solving problems; it's about experiencing them."

If we view life only in terms of problems, that is all we will see. But if we embrace life as an experience, we will enjoy every moment. Take care of moments, and moments will take care of you.

Problems are nothing but opportunities for creativity. Every challenge is a chance to showcase your unique skills and talents. If you're watching this video, type *"Problem Solving"* in the comment box. Writing it down will help reinforce the learning.

"You cannot drive out darkness with darkness; only light can do that."

– Martin Luther King Jr.

A problem is not a dead end; it is a guide leading you to the next step.

"No one has ever built a lock without a key. Similarly, no problem exists without a solution."

Imagine this: How long can you keep banging your head against a wall? Until you bleed? But the wall will never give way. Instead of wasting energy, use your mind to find another way.

"How long will you curse your fate? And how long will you sit under a mango tree expecting an orange?"

Crying over a problem will not solve it. Finding a way out of it will.

"Those who believe in solving problems will actively work toward solutions."

Problem-solving is the process of identifying a problem, understanding its cause, evaluating solutions, selecting the best option, and implementing it. It is not just about working hard; it is about working smart.

Characteristics of Problem Solving

1. It has a clear goal.
2. It requires analyzing different available alternatives.
3. It is a process of selecting the best option.
4. It is a mental exercise that requires deep thinking.
5. It involves logical decision-making for long-term well-being.

Types of Problems

*   Family problems – Relationships among family members can be complex, and handling differences with understanding is crucial.
*   Financial problems – Managing income, saving wisely, and investing smartly can help tackle financial issues.
*   Relationship problems – Spouse conflicts, parent-child struggles, and generational gaps need careful handling.
*   Health problems – Chronic illnesses and mental health challenges can make life difficult. A balanced lifestyle can help manage these issues.
*   Social problems – The society around us affects our lives. It's important to navigate social dynamics wisely.
*   Career-related problems – Workplace challenges, relationships with colleagues, and job stress need attention.
*   Environmental problems – Issues like pollution, waste management, and climate change impact everyone.
*   Intellectual problems – Engaging in debates, discussions, and creative thinking helps broaden perspectives.

"A problem is not a problem; it is the way you perceive it."

Nobody is perfect. Everyone faces struggles, but those who learn to live with them are the ones who succeed.

Famous People Who Overcame Challenges

- Abraham Lincoln faced many failures but eventually became the President of the United States in 1860.
- Albert Einstein couldn't speak until four years old and struggled with reading until seven, but he went on to win the Nobel Prize.
- Charles Darwin was called lazy and unfit by his father, yet he became the father of modern biology.
- J.K. Rowling was rejected by nine publishers before her *Harry Potter* books made her one of the world's richest authors.
- Ludwig van Beethoven was told he would never succeed in music, yet he became a legendary composer even after losing his hearing.
- Walt Disney was fired from a newspaper for "lack of imagination" but later created one of the biggest entertainment empires.
- Sudha Chandran lost her leg in an accident but became a famous dancer with an artificial limb.

The lesson? Obstacles do not define you; your response to them does.

"Problem-solving is an intellectual process."

Education is not about memorizing facts; it is about training the brain to think critically.

"The mind is like a parachute; it works only when it is open."

If you see problems as problems, that's all they will be. But if you see them as opportunities, they will open doors for you.

Final Thought:

"We all have problems. But how we solve them is what makes us unique."

So, what do you think? Start seeing challenges as opportunities, and success will follow!

4B.

Analytical Capability

By Jayaprakash Nagathihalli

Analyzing various situations and scenarios is very important. That's why I am sharing this crucial topic with you today. Let's try to understand the significance of analytical capability. There are numerous benefits to having strong analytical skills. It helps us in creative activities, whether painting or any other constructive work.

What is Analysis?

Essay writing is a great example of analytical ability. When writing an essay, we need to break down the subject by asking key questions:

- What?
- Where?
- Why?
- When?
- Who?
- How?

For instance, many of us have visited Jog Falls, but long ago, Sir M. Visvesvaraya looked at the falls and remarked, *"What a waste!"* He then suggested building a hydroelectric power plant, which was eventually constructed. Today, it generates 1100 MW of electricity.

The Power of Thought

- Digesting what we consume: Just like food needs to be digested for nourishment, thoughts must be processed for clear understanding.
- Understanding what we read: Simply reading is not enough; comprehending and interpreting in our own words is essential.

Definitions of Analysis

1. Breaking down a given situation or scenario into smaller parts and evaluating it logically.
2. Analyzing different aspects of a scenario is crucial for leading an effective life.
3. Win-Win thinking fosters teamwork, while Win-Loss thinking creates rivalry.

Who are the Best Analysts?

1. Mothers and their children – A mother understands her child's language and emotions.
2. Teachers and students – Educators strive to make students grasp the subject.
3. Mentors and disciples – In any field, mentors guide their disciples.
4. Speakers and audiences – A connection is formed between a speaker and listeners.

5. Musicians and listeners – Thousands gather to enjoy
    music.
6. Dramatists and viewers – Performers captivate
    audiences through acting.

Role of the Brain in Analysis

The left brain is responsible for:

- Logic
- Reasoning
- Analysis
- Calculations
- Realism

The right brain handles:

- Creativity
- Colors
- Imagination
- Emotions
- Intuition

Different Types of Analysis

Examples of scientific analysis:

- Classical Science (Traditional)
- Natural Science
- Pure Science
- Modern Science
- Spiritual Science

Stages of Analysis on Death

1. Denial – The refusal to accept reality.
2. Anger – Frustration over the loss.
3. Bargaining – Trying to negotiate a way out.
4. Depression – Sinking into sadness.
5. Acceptance – Coming to terms with reality.

Aspects of Personality Development

1. Physical Health
2. Mental Health
3. Emotional Well-being
4. Spiritual Health

Four Types of Functional Capabilities

1. Sensing – Awareness of surroundings.
2. Intuition – Knowing things before they happen.
3. Thinking – Processing thoughts logically.
4. Feeling – Managing emotions.

Skills That Enhance Analytical Ability

- General Skills
- Technical Skills
- Life Skills
- Critical Thinking Skills

Development of Skills

Skills begin at birth and evolve through:

1. Motor skills – Physical coordination.
2. Cognitive skills – Understanding and reasoning.
3. Social development skills – Building interpersonal relationships.

Key Life Skills

- Critical Analysis – Learning the ability to compare and evaluate.
- Creative Thinking – Developing artistic and innovative abilities.
- Problem-Solving – Becoming a part of the solution, not the problem.
- Decision Making – Knowing what choices to make and what to avoid.
- Communication Skills – Effective interaction with people.
- Interpersonal Relationships – Maintaining good social bonds.
- Self-Realization – Understanding oneself.
- Empathy – Putting oneself in another's position.
- Stress Management – Handling life pressures.
- Emotional Regulation – Managing emotions appropriately.

Five Tips to Improve Analytical Skills

1. Ask the right questions.
2. Acknowledge what you don't know.
3. Avoid making assumptions.
4. Don't take things at face value.
5. Transform information into knowledge.

For instance, the word *Imperfect* can also be read as *"I'm Perfect"* because everyone is perfect in their own unique ways.

At *Transformation Unlimited*, we conduct online and offline training sessions to enhance public speaking and life skills. Analytical ability is a subject close to my heart. When we understand the power of thought, we begin to see life from a unique perspective, making it more meaningful and insightful.

4C.

Elevate and Uplift

With V.R. Satyanarayana – Interview by Jayaprakash Nagathihalli

We often hear people say, "You haven't changed a bit in the last five or ten years!" We also observe some people who, for the past twenty years, have been discussing the same topics and ideas without any evolution. While time races forward, some individuals remain stagnant.

Why am I setting this context? Because if we don't update or upgrade ourselves, we will be left behind in this fast-paced world. Today, we are discussing the importance of upgrading. Any questions you have should be related to self-improvement and personal growth. To discuss this crucial subject, we have business expert V.R. Satyanarayana with us.

V.R. Satyanarayana is the founder of V.R. Consumer World Private Limited, Consumes Life Empowering, and SP Home Foods. He is an entrepreneur, a business consultant, a marathon runner, and a mentor who has helped many people grow their businesses through training programs.

Why is Upgradation Important?

Satyanarayana:

The fundamental principle of life is that anything that does not change remains stagnant, and anything stagnant eventually perishes. Upgradation is a natural process in life and nature. Everything progresses naturally—be it technology, society, or time itself. When we evolve with change, life becomes more fulfilling, businesses become successful, and relationships become more enjoyable. Otherwise, we risk becoming outdated and irrelevant in an advancing world.

Jayaprakash:

To explain the upgrade more clearly, let's take transportation as an example. It has evolved tremendously over time. Could you elaborate on that?

Satyanarayana:

Certainly! In the past, transportation was limited to walking. Then came the invention of the wheel, followed by carts, then engines, and finally, airplanes. Today, we can travel across countries within hours. Despite this progress, some people still claim that advancements are slow. But the reality is, transportation has evolved drastically, making our lives much easier.

Jayaprakash:

Human development itself has undergone massive changes. This program aims at personality development, which implies that humans need to adapt to changing times.

Satyanarayana:

Absolutely! We evolved from apes to modern humans through continuous development. Today, we witness great advancements in various fields, proving that upgradation is essential for survival and success.

The Evolution of Communication

Jayaprakash:

A great example of rapid progress is communication. A mobile phone was once just for calling, but now it takes photos, records videos, and provides internet access.

With smartphones having dual cameras and countless features, communication has advanced significantly.

Satyanarayana:
Intelligence is what sets humans apart from other species. Our intelligence helps us optimize resources and improve communication. In ancient times, we relied on pigeons to deliver messages. Then came the telegram, telephone, landline, and now

mobile phones, which have revolutionized communication. This is a perfect example of continuous upgradation.

Saraf, Bhatkal:

To upgrade one's personality, I recall a statement by the poet Bendre: *"You must constantly refine and improve yourself. To write well, you must first learn properly."* This applies to all fields—whether business or personal growth. Success and failure should be taken positively as part of learning.

Satyanarayana:

That's an excellent example. Upgradation requires effort and persistence. Many successful entrepreneurs faced multiple failures before achieving success. Growth happens only through continuous attempts.

The Role of Upgradation in Health and Lifestyle

K.J. Ratna, Mandya:

We see personal development happening, but modern lifestyles have also brought health problems. In the past, people were physically active, doing chores manually. Today, machines have taken over, leading to a decline in physical strength. This has made people more mechanical and dependent on technology.

Satyanarayana:

Despite technological advancements, maintaining fundamental human habits is crucial. In our training programs, we emphasize the importance of health, meditation, family time, and daily learning. We call this the Power Hour—an hour dedicated to self-improvement. Traditional lifestyles involved more physical work, but today, with automation, we need to consciously maintain an active lifestyle to stay healthy.

Jayaprakash:

We shouldn't become too dependent on machines. Some people say that today we love machines but use people, whereas it should be the other way around—we should love people and use machines.

Satyanarayana:

If we start loving machines too much, we might end up overburdening them while losing touch with human interaction. Parents often complain that their children's health is declining compared to previous generations. The key is balance—using technology wisely without becoming completely dependent on it.

Success Through Upgradation

Amaresh Dinni, Kavitala:

It takes five years to achieve success but just a minute to fall. Upgradation is good, but rapid success is not always sustainable. Farmers, for example, remain farmers all their lives, while some businessmen become rich quickly. What are your thoughts on this?

Satyanarayana:

That's a valid point, but I would argue that the idea of a farmer staying a farmer forever is outdated. Farmers today are leveraging modern technology like tractors, drones, and advanced irrigation methods. Those who stick to old ways get stuck, but those who upgrade themselves thrive. Over the last few decades, human intelligence has grown exponentially, and opportunities have increased tremendously. Those who upgrade themselves succeed.

Guiding Youth in a Changing World

Baburao Kulkarni, Vijayapura:

In the past, great leaders and role models inspired the youth. But in today's polluted social environment, how can young people develop a strong character?

Jayaprakash:

Corruption and negativity have always existed. The key is to focus on the positive influences around us.

Satyanarayana:

Yes! With today's communication technology, we are more aware of societal issues. But there are also many great leaders, ethical business people, and organizations doing amazing work. The youth should be exposed to positive role models and value-based education. We should promote good values and help spread awareness about self-improvement.

Upgradation vs. Generation Gap

Muralidhar, Rajajinagar:

What is the relationship between upgradation and the generation gap?

Satyanarayana:

The generation gap occurs when one generation fails to adapt to the next. If older generations resist change while younger generations move forward, a gap forms. However, when people continuously upgrade themselves, this gap can be minimized. Learning is a lifelong process. If we embrace change and stay updated, we remain connected across generations.

Final Thoughts

Upgradation is not just about adopting new technology—it's about personal, professional, and emotional growth. The world is evolving rapidly, and those who embrace continuous learning and self-improvement will thrive. Keep upgrading, keep evolving!

Jayaprakash:

What has happened today is that the concept of a "generation" has changed. Earlier, we used to say a generation was 30-40 years, but today, in just 5-10 years, or even less, things are changing drastically.

Satyanarayana:

Recently, we attended a social media workshop. In the next three years, we won't even need to think about five or ten years down the line. Today, if we look at technological advancements, the generational gap is not what it used to be. Instead of asking what changed in the last five years, we should be asking how things were six months ago. Even in the last three months, our country's economic system has changed drastically. Today, even vegetable vendors are using mobile apps for digital transactions. Financial systems have transformed. Technology is advancing at a rate I can't even imagine. In just six months, or even three months, generations are evolving. Jobs, businesses, and the future itself are being reshaped by artificial intelligence. AI is taking over. Whether we go to a hospital or any other industry, robots are beginning to replace human workers. In many places, robots are already doing jobs.

Jayaprakash:

What we need to understand here is that older generations must adapt to new developments and trends. It is inevitable.

Usha, Mysore:

As technology advances, writing and literacy seem to be declining. I sometimes wonder if an intelligent human even exists anymore. Work is getting done faster, but laziness is increasing among people.

Jayaprakash:

That might seem true, madam, but if you observe, publications are still thriving. Many books are continuously being published, and people are still reading them. Just because something appears to be declining, it doesn't mean it's entirely true. You're asking if writing is decreasing.

Satyanarayana:

Look at what's happening today—many bookstores are still running successfully. Publishing houses continue to operate. The need for "touch and feel" remains, even in this digital age. Even though online shopping is available, people still prefer visiting physical stores to see products. The same applies to books—people still like to pick up and read physical books. Technology can help bridge the gap where needed. With advancements like virtual reality, we can now sit in one place and experience another country without physically going there.

Arun, Electronic City:

Farmers are considered the backbone of the country, yet they are committing suicide. If this backbone keeps breaking, will it survive? How can farmers be uplifted?

Jayaprakash:

Even farmers have opportunities for advancement. Many farmers are now growing commercial crops instead of traditional farming. Some young people are even moving back to villages, realizing that agriculture is more profitable than some urban jobs. We see people leaving the city due to heavy traffic and moving to rural areas to work in farming.

Satyanarayana:

Let me give you an example. A young entrepreneur named Srinath from the company Consumax started an agro-business called "Hosa Chiguru" and is now farming on 1,000 acres using advanced technology. He mentioned that many young people are now getting into farming.

Jayaprakash:

That means the trend is changing, and we need to notice this shift. People often think technology is causing problems, but it depends on how we use it. A knife, for example, can be used to harm someone or to cut an apple—it all depends on how we use it. Similarly, we must use technology wisely.

Chetan Kumar, Tiptur:

Farmers are feeling helpless. They lack the capability to integrate technology.

Jayaprakash:

Many farmers' children are moving to cities. But if they acquire knowledge and skills, they can stand on their own feet and return to support their villages. There are so many possibilities.

Satyanarayana:

That was a good question. Saying farmers lack capability is not entirely true. Every human is born with potential. Whether it's a bicycle shop owner, a mechanic, or a small trader—everyone has the ability to develop their skills. When someone starts thinking about how to improve and innovate in their field, they begin to grow. Let me give my own example: when I started my business at 18, I had no resources, no financial backing, no speaking skills, and no strong personality. But I started asking, "What can I do?" I didn't remain a frog in the well.

Jayaprakash:

Many of us think like that—underestimating ourselves. It's not about overestimating ourselves, but self-analysis is key, isn't it?

Satyanarayana:

Self-analysis is important, but so is learning from others. There will always be someone in our town or village who has done better. Instead of feeling jealous, we should ask, "How did they succeed?" and learn from them.

Jayaprakash:

Many people don't even knock on the doors of government offices to inquire about available schemes or new agricultural developments. There are agricultural universities and various programs available to help farmers. If we stay informed, we can take our work to the next level.

Satyanarayana:

Yes, upgrading is essential. If we don't upgrade ourselves, we remain stagnant like still water, which eventually gets contaminated. But if we keep flowing like a river, we remain fresh and useful. Similarly, when a person upgrades their knowledge, skills, and mindset, they grow along with society and business. That makes life beautiful. Those who stop upgrading begin to struggle.

Gopal, Belagavi:

Isn't personality development just about becoming rich?

Jayaprakash:

Becoming wealthy is one aspect, but it's not the only goal. Who wouldn't want money? But personality development has multiple dimensions. Can you elaborate on this?

Satyanarayana:

Personality development isn't just about making money. Let me give a powerful example. What is the most dominant species that ever lived on Earth? Most people would say dinosaurs. But despite their enormous size, they became extinct. Meanwhile, cockroaches, which are tiny, have survived for millions of years. Why? Because they adapted and upgraded to their surroundings. This is why upgrading is important—not just to become rich, but to live a well-rounded, happy life.

Jayaprakash:

Even poor people can become rich if they upgrade themselves.

Hari, Malleshwaram:

Upgradation is nothing but change. But there's a lot of unhealthy competition today. We need higher values, not just shortcuts. "Choose the best and leave the rest." There's even a saying by Sarvajna: "More than a million skills, the skill of farming is supreme." What do you think?

Jayaprakash:

Absolutely true. Farmers are essential. We all need food, and that's only possible because of them. You mentioned, "Choose the best and leave the rest"—if we consistently choose the best things in life and let go of unnecessary burdens, wouldn't our lives be so much better?

Satyanarayana:

We need to upgrade while maintaining our values. Upgradation should not mean losing our cultural and familial values. When children go to good schools, they learn new things, but as parents, we must also upgrade ourselves. Otherwise, we might feel disconnected from them. If a child comes home excited about learning something new, and we don't understand it, they will start feeling distant from us. If we upgrade ourselves, we can connect better with them.

Shivaprakash, Haveri:

ATMs deduct charges if we withdraw more than four times a month. Doesn't this affect farmers, especially in rural areas where ATMs are scarce?

Jayaprakash:

There are systems in place, and every country has rules that we need to follow. Farmers are also adapting. We once thought people wouldn't accept demonetization, but they did, didn't they?

Satyanarayana:

That's the whole point of this discussion—if we don't upgrade, we will be left behind. We must continuously work on improving ourselves.

Jayaprakash:

We must also focus on improving our businesses...

Conversation on Leadership, Change, and Personal Growth

Satyanarayana:

Leadership is about uplifting everyone toward positive change. In my opinion, leaders are the primary drivers of transformation.

Jayaprakash:

They hold a guiding light ahead, leading the way while inviting others to follow. This act of calling people to the right path is crucial.

Satyanarayana:

They serve as beacons, illuminating the way for others.

Jayaprakash:

Doesn't this mean that society itself undergoes transformation when leaders guide it in the right direction?

Satyanarayana:

Absolutely. Leaders bear the responsibility of steering society toward progress. Leadership is fundamentally an accountable role. Throughout history, different leaders have shaped society for the better.

Jayaprakash:

Earlier, you mentioned that people shouldn't be like frogs in a well, stuck in stagnation. Why is that?

Satyanarayana:

Because life is beautiful, and we shouldn't restrict our vision. If we limit ourselves, it's like putting blinders on a horse—it only sees what's in front. While focus is necessary—like students dedicating themselves to studies or entrepreneurs staying committed until they achieve success—it's also important to be open to new experiences.

Jayaprakash:

If we stay focused while moving forward, wouldn't we experience transformations in life, like witnessing waterfalls and rainbows along the journey?

Satyanarayana:

Yes! As we progress, we encounter new perspectives. If we blindly keep moving with tunnel vision, we might miss the beauty of the waterfall. But if we look around and take it all in, we can enjoy the journey. Our goal should be to elevate our awareness to the next level.

Jayaprakash:

Our outlook on life shapes our journey. How do perspective and personal growth connect?

Satyanarayana:

Here's an example: A teacher once told students they must get top marks. But when the students questioned why six different subjects required six different teachers, yet they were expected to excel in all, it shifted the perspective. Today, thinking has evolved.

Those who remain neutral in learning must upgrade their way of seeing life, society, and business.

Jayaprakash:

Many parents complain that kids waste time on mobile phones. But if they use them for education or business growth via social media, wouldn't it lead to positive change?

Satyanarayana:

Exactly! I recently spoke with someone who reflected on how, in the past, they could only meet relatives during family functions. But now, technology enables 24/7 connectivity. While it's beneficial, we must control technology instead of letting it control us.

Jayaprakash:

It's like using a remote control—we should command it, not the other way around. Many people live a monotonous life—work, home, TV, and sleep. How important is it to break that routine?

Satyanarayana:

Taking breaks is essential. When we pause, we engage in self-reflection. Even in my training programs, I take breaks every few months to relax, rejuvenate, and upgrade my skills.

Jayaprakash:

Just like Sundays provide a weekly break, periodic reflection helps break monotony. What are the benefits of breaking stagnation?

Satyanarayana:

A stagnant mind is like a frog in a well—it sees nothing beyond its small world. When we take breaks, we cut through that condition. Training programs, mentors, and self-awareness help us break free from monotony.

Jayaprakash:

Having an open mind is key, as the Rigveda says: "Let noble thoughts come to us from all directions." How does one cultivate an open mind?

Satyanarayana:

By taking breaks! When we step away from routine, we make space for new thoughts. A relaxed mind is more open and creative.

Ramesh (Rajajinagar):

Many people want to embrace new things but struggle because their minds resist change.

Jayaprakash:

That's where the concept of "unlearning" comes in. We often hear about learning, but what does unlearning mean?

Satyanarayana:

Unlearning is about letting go of outdated habits. It's like moving from typewriters to computers. If we cling to old methods, we can't progress. Learning requires upgrading knowledge, and unlearning helps us break rigid patterns.

Jayaprakash:

How does training help in this process?

Satyanarayana:

Training programs play a crucial role in personality development. In the past, stories from scriptures helped people grow. Today, training workshops fulfill that purpose.

Jayaprakash:

Have people truly transformed through such training programs?

Satyanarayana:

I am a living example. Eighteen years ago, I felt like a failure. Today, I have guided thousands. Training accelerates change by making unlearning easier.

Srinivas (KR Puram):

Many people attend personality development programs but fail to change their behavior. Why is that?

Jayaprakash:

Learning is one thing, but practicing it is another. Satyanarayana attended training and now leads four companies. He applied what he learned—that's why he succeeded. Practice is key!

Satyanarayana:

Exactly! Personality development isn't just about external behavior. Internal transformation must happen first. Training workshops don't create instant change, but they lay the foundation for long-term growth.

Jayaprakash:

Like public speaking training—you see immediate results when someone who feared speaking in the morning confidently delivers a speech by evening.

Satyanarayana:

Some changes are visible quickly, while others take time. Personal growth is a continuous process.

Jayaprakash:

With evolving trends, how do we adapt and stay relevant?

Satyanarayana:

Just like WhatsApp and Facebook get constant updates, we must also upgrade ourselves. Adapting to new trends ensures continuous growth.

Jayaprakash:

How do successful leaders embrace change and keep improving?

Satyanarayana:

True leaders never stop evolving. They don't settle after one achievement; they always look for what's next. That's what keeps them at the top.

Jayaprakash:

I've noticed a rise in mentors and counselors. How do mentors help individuals grow?

Satyanarayana:

Mentors guide individuals beyond their self-imposed limits. They help people recognize their potential and build confidence. When knowledge increases, so does courage.

Jayaprakash:

And with courage, people move forward in life. How important is skill development alongside this?

Satyanarayana:

Mentors not only provide knowledge but also emphasize practice. Skills must be continuously honed to remain competitive.

This conversation highlights the importance of leadership, adaptability, and continuous self-improvement in personal and professional life

5.

Emotional Mirror

Emotional Personality

*"Something that cannot be valued in money,
but can only be experienced,
is emotional personality and
the ladder to happiness."*

— Jayaprakash Nagathihalli

The greatest journey in life is the one that moves from the brain to the heart. It is a small transition from thoughts to emotions. The physical distance between the brain and heart is about 14 inches, but emotionally, this journey is profound. Emotional personality helps establish a strong connection between the heart and mind, thereby enhancing a person's competence and dedication.

Love, affection, bonding, friendship, trust, empathy, and the sense of universal humanity introduce our personality to others. A smiling face, harmony, speaking only when necessary, considering oneself as part of a whole, and humility make one stand out from others.

ಭಾವನಾತ್ಮಕ ಜೀವನ

Emotional personality includes the ability to manage and express emotions like joy, sorrow, and anger. It allows a person to understand the depths of their own emotions and recognize and reflect on the emotions of others effectively.

Key Aspects of Emotional Personality

1. Understanding Emotions – The ability to recognize and comprehend one's own and others' emotions.
2. Expressing Emotions – The ability to articulate emotions appropriately and effectively.
3. Emotional Control – The ability to regulate and manage emotions wisely.
4. Maintaining Relationships – Using emotional intelligence to build and sustain meaningful relationships.
5. Accountability – Taking responsibility for one's emotions and making thoughtful decisions.

The Importance of Emotional Personality

Emotional personality plays a crucial role in personal and professional life.

1. Communication & Connection – Enhances one's ability to communicate and establish strong bonds with others.
2. Expressing Thoughts Clearly – Helps in articulating emotions and opinions effectively.
3. Inner Happiness – Boosts self-awareness and overall well-being.
4. Self-Confidence – Allows individuals to understand themselves better and express their emotions freely.
5. Relationship Management – Strengthens social bonds, friendships, and family relationships.

6. Personal Influence – Makes one's personality more powerful and appealing, increasing their credibility and respect.

Ways to Enhance Emotional Personality

Developing emotional intelligence is a gradual process. Here are some effective methods to improve it:

1. Self-Reflection – Take time to understand your emotions and analyze why you feel a certain way.
2. Expressing Emotions – Do not hesitate to share your emotions through writing, speaking, or art.
3. Self-Observation – Observe how you react in different situations and assess your responses.
4. Empathy – Try to understand others' emotions by putting yourself in their shoes.
5. Commitment & Determination – Focus on developing emotional intelligence with dedication.
6. Practices Like Yoga & Meditation – Helps in calming the mind and balancing emotions.
7. Effective Communication – Learn communication skills that help in expressing emotions constructively.
8. Building Positive Relationships – Strengthen relationships with supportive and encouraging individuals.
9. Training & Learning – Attend workshops or courses that improve emotional intelligence and social skills.

Notable Quotes on Emotional Personality

1. **Maya Angelou** – *"People may not remember what you said or did, but they will always remember how you made them feel."*
2. **Carl Rogers** – *"Knowing oneself and one's emotions is the best way to understand personality."*
3. **Daniel Goleman** – *"Emotional intelligence is a key factor in personal and professional success."*
4. **Brené Brown** – *"Expressing emotions is a sign of strength; sharing them helps us grow."*
5. **Rollo May** – *"Emotions have the power to shape or break our lives. They define our experiences."*
6. **Eleanor Roosevelt** – *"No one can make you feel inferior without your consent."*
7. **Mahatma Gandhi** – *"When emotions align with truth and faith, we gain immense strength."*

Impact of Emotions on Life

Emotions play a powerful role in shaping a person's personal, social, and professional life. Some key influences include:

1. Inner Happiness – Enhances overall well-being and mental peace.
2. Relationships – Strengthens social and personal bonds.
3. Health – Positive emotions contribute to better physical and mental health.
4. Decision Making – Helps in making wise and thoughtful decisions.
5. Excellence & Motivation – Encourages self-growth and higher achievements.

6. Equality – Promotes empathy and understanding among people.
7. Critical Thinking – Fosters deep and insightful thoughts.

Final Thought

"Love people, use things.
True happiness lies in our emotional richness."

— Jayaprakash Nagathihalli

5A.

Emotions

An Interview with Mysore Ramakrishna Ravishankar, Spiritual Guide,

by Jayaprakash Nagathihalli

Jayaprakash Nagathihalli:

Namaskara.
Welcome to the *Vyaktitva Darpana* (Personality Mirror) program, which attempts to hold up a mirror to our personality

and reflect on whether we can transform our lives. One thing we must always remember is that *we are the sculptors of our own lives*.

Today's topic is *Emotions*. Every day, everyone experiences a range of emotions. Hence, emotions shape our personality. That is undeniable. People say, *The key to happiness is to always have control over your emotions*. In other words, if we desire happiness, it is crucial to regulate our emotions. Good emotions pave the way to happiness. Cultivating and nurturing emotions is our own responsibility.

Controlling our emotions is very important. Adapting every situation to suit ourselves is in our hands. It is often said that *the entire world is full of emotions*. One could say that emotions function like computer software, and that wouldn't be wrong.

Everything appears as per our emotions. They influence our physical state and our speech. Today, we have with us Mysore Ramakrishna Ravishankar, a spiritual guide, to discuss emotions and how they can change our lives. He is also addressed as *Mahacharya Ravishankar Ji*.

Ravishankar Ji, welcome to the *Vyaktitva Darpana* program. The word *Emotions* is something we use often. We hear about *songs filled with emotion*. We also notice emotions on people's faces and begin to interpret them. So, what is the true significance of emotions?

Ravishankar:

Namaskara. Before I answer, you mentioned that the world is filled with emotions. The entire universe appears as we perceive it. The way we manage our emotions directly influences how we see the world. That is why emotions are so important. Everything starts from there. We must constantly observe whether we are influencing emotions or being influenced by them. This awareness is crucial.

Jayaprakash:

The name of our program is *Vyaktitva Darpana* (Personality Mirror). What we see in the world is our reflection. So, in a way, emotions serve as a mirror, don't they?

Ravishankar:

You put it perfectly. Before we go out, we look in a mirror, don't we? To check how we appear. Similarly, we have an inner mirror that reflects who we truly are. Your show has been given a wonderful name. *Vyaktitva Darpana*—a mirror for our personality. It is essential to assess our own personality. The way we perceive ourselves determines how we perceive the world.

Jayaprakash:

For instance, if we meet someone, we see them based on our emotions. How we see them and how they respond to us is determined by our emotions, right?

Ravishankar:

Absolutely. If you step out with a smiling face, everyone you meet in the morning will greet you with smiles. But if you go out looking upset, people will ask, *What happened?* This is a natural process. We all do this. Because the world reflects our emotions, we must first change our emotions.

Jayaprakash:

We tend to categorize people based on roles. For example, when we see a woman, we interpret her identity in different ways. Could you elaborate on that?

Ravishankar:

When someone sees a woman, one person may think of her as their mother, another as their wife, another as their sister, and another as a friend. The same woman is seen from different perspectives based on emotions. The person doesn't change, but the way they are perceived does. That perception is what we call *emotion*.

Jayaprakash:

There is a saying, *People see others based on their own emotions and devotion.* That means the way we see the world is shaped by our perspective. The influence of emotions is crucial. We see smiles, love, anger, patience, faith, attachment, jealousy, and ego.

Ravishankar:

Yes. No single emotion is permanent. We continuously change. But the key is how we respond to situations. If someone is grieving, and we walk in laughing, it wouldn't be appropriate. We must align our emotions with the situation. It is important to recognize whether we control our emotions or let them control us.

People say we should always be happy. But sometimes, crying is also important. If one cries wholeheartedly, the heaviness in the heart lightens. Many people try to console others by telling them not to cry. But truly, experiencing emotions fully can bring relief.

Jayaprakash:

If we want to understand life, we must recognize which emotions are beneficial—such as devotion, love, friendship, and service. These qualities bring balance and contentment, making life beautiful.

Ravishankar:

That's a great question. What do we all seek in life? Happiness. Even crying serves a purpose—because after crying, we feel relieved. So ultimately, everyone wants happiness. But happiness is an experience, and emotions determine that experience. If we embrace emotions like devotion, we will find deep happiness.

Jayaprakash:

We have a caller, Rajanagowda. Please ask your question.

Rajanagowda:

Namaskara, sir. Understanding emotions is very important in shaping personality. In theater, for example, an actor expresses emotions that entertain the audience, whether it's humor or sorrow. Emotions play a crucial role in acting. Thank you for sharing your insights.

Jayaprakash:

That was a great point. To act in a play, one must express emotions, right? Without immersing oneself in a role, one cannot convey it effectively.

Ravishankar:

Exactly. If an actor plays Ravana, they must truly *feel* like Ravana. Otherwise, their portrayal will feel fake. Audiences will notice the difference between the real person and the actor. True acting requires *parakaya pravesha*—entering the role completely. That's the essence of emotion.

Jayaprakash:

We have another caller, Amaresh Dinni. Please ask your question.

Amaresh Dinni:

Sir, is there an inseparable connection between emotions and pain? People often say, *I no longer have feelings for you.* When this happens, doesn't it hurt? If emotions disappear, doesn't that lead to pain? Or should we avoid emotions to avoid pain?

Ravishankar:

That's an excellent question. Pain is an experience resulting from emotions. However, emotions and experiences are different. Pain arises from how we hold onto emotions. People have the freedom to feel their own emotions, just as you have the freedom to feel yours. The moment we realize that pain is not caused by others but by our own emotional attachment, we begin to let go. Awareness and understanding help pain fade away.

Jayaprakash:

We have one more caller, Manjunath from Mysore. Please ask your question.

Manjunath:

We have attended your classes. We learned that we express emotions to others, but they may not always respond the way we expect. Emotions vary. How should we navigate such situations in life?

Ravishankar:

That is a very good question. It is really well thought out. You are asking very insightful questions. The viewers are very perceptive. First, I must thank them because their questions lead to meaningful discussions.

Yes, what they mentioned is true—each of us perceives the world in our own unique way. The world I see is not the same as the world you see. This is because we experience the world through our own emotions and thoughts. Essentially, we create our own world. The very meaning of the world is that it is what we perceive and construct within ourselves. Without us, there is no world.

When we don't see or experience something, we may feel a sense of unease. However, we must learn to present our world in the best way possible. Some of you are very aware and insightful. When people come to you and interact with you, if you give them a certain emotional experience, they will learn from it. This is the next level of understanding.

First Level – Understanding ourselves and our own perception of the world. Observing whether the world we desire exists or not. Next Level – Connecting with others and helping them align with our perspective.

Without training, difficulties arise.

Jayaprakash:

Ravishankar ji, let's talk about troubling emotions. What are the emotions that cause distress? Hatred, betrayal, jealousy, and mistakes we repeatedly make—these are all part of what we call Kama (desire), Lobha (greed), Mada (pride), and Moha (attachment). How should we keep these troubling emotions in check?

Ravishankar:

These are known as the six internal enemies (Arishadvargas)— Kama (desire), Krodha (anger), Moha (delusion), Mada (pride), and Matsarya (envy). They all exist within our emotions.

Whenever we hold onto these emotions, we begin to recognize their impact. How? If you feel anger or hatred towards someone, you will notice physical changes in your body. Your speech, movements, and behavior change. We must observe these changes. The moment we start paying attention, transformation begins.

Most of the time, we don't observe ourselves. If someone says, "You seem angry, try to calm down," we tend to react instead of responding. A wise person, however, recognizes these emotions before they take over. The more we understand ourselves, the more control we gain over our emotions.

There are different types of emotions:

- Concepts and perceptions
- Feelings and sentiments
- Thought processes, consciousness, and awareness
- Spirituality and energy

For example, the way we think influences how we feel. If we keep thinking about something repeatedly, it forms an emotion. If we continuously speak about someone, over time, we develop a feeling about them—whether they are good, trustworthy, or likable.

Thus, emotions shape our experiences.

Jayaprakash:

We got a call from Dharwad. Srikanth is calling. Srikanth, please ask your question.

Srikanth:

Sir, Guruji often says that emotions play a significant role in shaping an individual's personality. However, the environment also has a major influence.

For example, if twin babies are raised in two different environments—one in a spiritual monastery and the other in a rough neighborhood—over time, their behaviors will be different. The child in the monastery may learn prayers and mantras, while the child in the rough environment may learn aggression and harsh words.

Jayaprakash:

Yes, social sciences discuss this in depth. The influence of the environment cannot be ignored, can it?

Ravishankar:

If you plant a seed and nurture it properly, it will grow well. If you don't take care of it, it won't thrive. The type of seed you plant determines the plant that grows. The same principle applies to emotions. The emotions you cultivate will shape your character.

However, even in challenging environments, a strong inner self can emerge. Some people grow stronger despite hardships. It depends on how emotions are nurtured.

Srikanth:

Sir, I have another question. A few years ago, a movie called *Jarasandha* was released, featuring actor Duniya Vijay. The movie depicted a child who was born with violent tendencies and grew up to be a rowdy despite his mother's efforts to change him.

Jayaprakash:

It's difficult to analyze movies here. Films are written based on what appeals to the audience. But we are discussing the environment's impact on a person. If someone believes that their fate is predetermined from birth and cannot be changed, then what is the point of effort?

That's not true. Change is possible. If you think you can, you can. If you think you can't, you can't.

Ramesh (caller from Kavatagi):

Sir, if a person is deeply suffering mentally, how can they come out of it?

Ravishankar:

That is an excellent question, Ramesh.

One must come out of suffering because staying in pain indefinitely is not an option. Mental suffering is an emotional turmoil—it affects our body. It makes it difficult to walk, talk, or even function normally. Some people collapse under emotional stress because they cannot handle it. Their face changes, they sweat excessively, and their body reacts. In medicine, this is called psychosomatic—the mind affects the body.

There is a difference between emotions and emotional outbursts.

- Emotions can be consciously created and controlled.

- Emotional outbursts take over and control us.

For example, Love is an emotion. But when it turns into an uncontrollable obsession (e.g., "I can't live without you"), it becomes an emotional outburst. That's when people act impulsively or even think of harming themselves.

True love doesn't demand reciprocation. If you love someone, it should be unconditional. Love should not turn into possessiveness. When we recognize this, we can be loving towards everyone without attachment.

Our thoughts shape our emotions.

- A simple thought can lead to a possibility.
- A possibility turns into an experience.
- That experience reinforces our belief.

If we believe something is impossible, it remains impossible. If we believe it is possible, we work towards making it happen.

This is why emotions and experiences are deeply interconnected.

Jayaprakash:

We have another caller, Prahlad. Please go ahead.

Prahlad:

Guruji, I have written a poem:

> ***"Oh mind, surrender to the divine,***
> ***Bow your head in humility.***

Find solace within yourself,
In the remembrance of the Supreme."

I have decided to live my life with this mindset.

Ravishankar:

Very nice!

In Sanskrit, there is a saying:

"Manah eva manushyanam karanam bandha
mokshayoh."

(*The mind alone is responsible for bondage or liberation.*)

Even if someone is physically imprisoned, if their mind is free, they do not feel trapped. On the other hand, someone who is mentally enslaved remains in suffering even when physically free.

The mind is like a vessel—it holds all our emotions. What we fill it with determines our life experience.

Adi Shankaracharya provided a step-by-step guide to transformation:

1. Satsang (good company) leads to detachment.
2. Detachment reduces worldly desires.
3. Freedom from desires brings stability.
4. Stability leads to liberation.

By carefully choosing and nurturing our emotions, we can shape our destiny. When we create art, poetry, or meaningful expressions from our emotions, it becomes a beautiful and fulfilling experience.

5B.

Mother's Love

Special Interview for Gauri Ganesh Festival – With Shrilatha

Jayaprakash Nagathihalli: Good morning and warm greetings to all our viewers on the occasion of the Gauri Ganesh festival. A heartfelt welcome to all to the *Vyaktitva Darpana* (Personality Mirror) program. This program is a small attempt to hold a mirror to our personality. As we explore various aspects of our personality, we can observe numerous changes within ourselves. By gradually incorporating these insights into our lives, transformation is inevitable. After all, *you are the creator of your own destiny.* There is no need to blame anyone else, because we are the architects of our own progress.

Dear viewers, as you all know, during the Gauri Ganesh festival, we learn a lot about Goddess Gauri and Lord Ganesha while celebrating the festival with devotion. Gauri represents motherhood, and Ganesha represents her son. This highlights the beautiful aspect of a mother's love. Today, in our *Vyaktitva Darpana* program, we are discussing this precious topic— *Mother's Love.* Who doesn't love their mother? This is a touching and heartwarming subject. To provide us with deeper insights on this, we have with us today personality development trainer *Shrilatha.* Shrilatha Ma'am, a warm welcome to our program.

Shrilatha: Thank you. Namaste.

Jayaprakash Nagathihalli: Ma'am, how would you like to convey your greetings to our viewers on this auspicious occasion of the Gauri Ganesh festival?

Shrilatha: *Vakratunda Mahakaya Suryakoti Samaprabha, Nirvighnam Kurume Deva Sarva Karyeshu Sarvada.* I bow to Lord Ganesha, the first-worshipped deity, the remover of obstacles, and the bestower of success. I extend my heartfelt greetings to all viewers for the Gauri Ganesh festival.

Jayaprakash: We always chant prayers like *Shuklambharadaram Vishnum, Shashivarnam Chaturbhujam, Prasanna Vadanam Dhyayeth, Sarva Vighnopa Shantaye* before starting any new task. Why is Lord Ganesha always remembered first?

Shrilatha: This tradition originates from the story of Goddess Parvati creating Lord Ganesha. When Parvati Devi went for a bath, Lord Shiva, unaware that Ganesha was his son, beheaded him. Later, when Parvati insisted on reviving him, Shiva attached the head of an elephant to Ganesha's body and blessed him, declaring that he must always be worshipped first before any endeavor.

Jayaprakash: That's true. This is why, during the Gauri Ganesh festival, we associate Ganesha with creativity.

Shrilatha: Absolutely, sir.

Jayaprakash: We have seen exhibitions featuring thousands of different Ganesha idols, each with a unique appearance. No matter how Ganesha is depicted, he always carries a distinct charm, doesn't he?

Shrilatha: Certainly, sir.

Jayaprakash: Creativity is essential. In this context, the power of Ganesha's creativity should also be highlighted, right?

Shrilatha: Of course, sir. Even from the making of a Ganesha idol, we can learn valuable life lessons. Every aspect of his form conveys a message.

Jayaprakash: Today, since we are talking about motherhood, let's connect it to Goddess Gauri. How does Gauri, as a mother, guide others?

Shrilatha: The Gauri festival is celebrated with great joy, symbolizing prosperity and auspiciousness. For Goddess Parvati, this is a festival of reunion with her parental home, which is why it holds a deep emotional significance for all mothers. It reminds every woman of her maternal home and strengthens family bonds.

Jayaprakash: Celebrating festivals is a way of bringing families together, isn't it?

Shrilatha: Yes, exactly. The festival signifies the eternal bond between a woman and her parental home. Every year, Parvati (also known as Gauri) visits her parents' home, where she is welcomed with offerings by married women seeking prosperity and marital bliss. Traditionally, a decorated mandap is set up, homes are adorned with mango leaves and rangoli, and married women exchange *Bagina* (a symbolic gift of prosperity).

Jayaprakash Nagathihalli: This festival is indeed celebrated with grandeur. When we worship Shiva, Parvati, and Ganesha, what spiritual or personal benefits does it bring to an individual?

Shrilatha: Festivals bring immense joy to the heart. In today's fast-paced life, people rarely find time to meet their relatives, but festivals provide an opportunity for families to reunite and celebrate together. They also help preserve cultural traditions and pass them on to the next generation.

Jayaprakash: Who can be considered as ideal mothers?

Shrilatha: If we look at history, *Yashoda* is regarded as an ideal mother in the *Dwapara Yuga*, as she lovingly raised Krishna, the savior of the world. Similarly, *Sita Devi*, *Renuka Devi*, and many other revered figures exemplify motherhood. Behind every great personality, there is always an ideal mother.

Jayaprakash Nagathihalli: That was beautifully said. Let's continue talking about *Mother's Love*. We all have a mother, and that is a special blessing. Without a mother, we wouldn't even exist in this world.

Shrilatha: Absolutely.

Jayaprakash: Why should we deeply reflect on a mother's love? Why is it so important to understand its significance?

Shrilatha: A mother's love is a divine force beyond measure. It is an unquantifiable, selfless energy that exists in every individual. If we compare a person to a flower bud, then a mother's love is like the sunlight that nurtures it to bloom. When we study the lives of great achievers, we always find the influence of an ideal mother behind their success.

[Caller from Talikoti – Chandragouda Kulkarni]
Chandragouda: Namaste, sir. Today's discussion on Gauri and Ganesha is wonderful. I would like to add that Ganesha is considered the first child of Mother Earth. Historically, after tending livestock, he was the first to cultivate land, making him the pioneer of agriculture. His bond with Mother Earth is deeper than any other. Could you elaborate on this aspect?

Shrilatha: Yes, indeed! Ganesha is often associated with Mother Earth, and there's a belief that our motherland is greater than even heaven. The connection between Ganesha and the Earth is symbolic of a nurturing relationship, just as a mother nourishes her child.

[Caller from Koppal – Mohan]
Mohan: There are so many orphaned children who lack a mother's love. How can we provide them with affection?

Jayaprakash: That is a very thoughtful question. Many organizations and individuals are stepping in to provide these children with a mother's care. But beyond institutions, we all can share motherly love with them through kindness and support. What are your thoughts?

Shrilatha: A mother's love is not confined to a biological mother. Anyone with a compassionate heart—be it caregivers in orphanages, teachers, or even friends—can offer motherly affection.

[Caller from Kavitala – Amaresh Dinni]

Amaresh: Greetings to both of you. *A mother's love gives me goosebumps just thinking about it!* I am my mother's only son. No matter what mistakes I make, my mother always defends me. Why do mothers always justify their children's actions?

Jayaprakash: That's a touching thought. A mother's love is unconditional, boundless, and forgiving. It is one of the purest forms of love.

Shrilatha: Indeed! A mother's love absorbs all pain, just as Ganesha's big belly symbolizes digesting life's hardships. Her patience, sacrifice, and forgiveness define her greatness.

Jayaprakash: This has been a wonderful discussion. Thank you, Shrilatha Ma'am, for sharing your insights on the beauty of *Mother's Love.*

Shrilatha: Thank you. Namaste.

Jayaprakash: The word "mother" itself evokes such deep emotions, and it's not wrong to say so. You even described a mother as the real god of everyone's life, full of love, kindness, and patience. Why did you use these words?

Srilatha: Because there's a saying that God cannot be everywhere, so He created mothers. The moment a child is born, they see the entire heaven or world through their mother's eyes. That's why I love to say that a mother is a true goddess.

Jayaprakash Nagathihalli: This is something we can observe even in animals and birds. The role of a mother is significant everywhere—whether in birds or animals—they fulfill their roles wholeheartedly.

Srilatha: Take a cat, for example. When a mother cat carries her kitten from one place to another, she holds it by the scruff of its neck. If we look at the kitten at that moment, it will be sleeping peacefully. Why? Because it has immense trust in its mother—it knows she won't drop it.

Jayaprakash: Absolutely. Let's take another call. Rajesh from Mumbai is calling. Rajesh, Namaste.

Rajesh: Namaste. In today's times, families are getting smaller. Earlier, we had joint families, but now nuclear families are increasing. People are less concerned about their extended relations and families. As a result, the sense of love and bonding is fading. What kind of awareness is needed today to redevelop this love? Because people are losing their sense of relationships.

Jayaprakash: That's a very important point, Rajesh. Bonding within families is reducing. When we had joint families, relationships were given more importance. But now, not as much. This program itself is an attempt to raise awareness about such issues. Today, people don't have anyone to talk to about their problems. We cannot talk to machines. Many people are living only on their mobiles or computers, and they miss out on real emotions. What do you think?

Srilatha: Earlier, we didn't have specialized counselors. Parents, grandparents, uncles, and aunts were always there to share our feelings. But in today's WhatsApp and Facebook era, we just send messages. However, without understanding the emotions behind these messages, counseling has become more necessary. That's why, at least during festivals and special occasions, if families come together and celebrate, it can help rcvive these lost relationships.

Jayaprakash: It's not just about sending messages...

Srilatha: It's about expressing emotions.

Jayaprakash: Expressing emotions is very important.

Srilatha: Absolutely.

Jayaprakash: It's not that we should remember our mothers only on Mother's Day, right?

Srilatha: Certainly not.

Jayaprakash: We should cherish these relationships every day. In our *Vyakthitva Darpana* program, we are discussing a mother's love. Ganesh Bhat from Kundapura is calling. Ganesh Bhat, Namaste.

Ganesh Bhat: Namaste, Madam.

Jayaprakash: Please ask your question, Ganesh Bhat.

Ganesh Bhat: Sir, I wish you both a very happy *Gauri Ganesh* festival.

Jayaprakash: Wishing you and everyone in the country the same. Please go ahead with your question.

Ganesh Bhat: Madam, my question is more of a thought. In every household, mothers love their children unconditionally. However, usually, sons are more attached to their mothers, while daughters are more attached to their fathers. Can you analyze this a little?

Jayaprakash: It's like saying *opposite poles attract each other*. What you observed is very true and insightful.

Srilatha: Certainly, sir. More than a reason, it is an emotional connection. Even though mothers love their daughters too, somewhere in their hearts, they believe that in their old age, their sons will take care of them. That could be one of the reasons.

Jayaprakash: That's an interesting perspective. We have another caller, Usha from Mysore. Usha, Namaste.

Usha: Namaste to both of you.

Jayaprakash: Namaste.

Usha: Madam, you are speaking so beautifully and sweetly. I can see the image of Goddess Gauramma in you today.

Jayaprakash: You see the image of Gauramma in her?

Usha: Absolutely, she is explaining things so well.

Jayaprakash: Okay, okay.

Usha: I wanted to share something. As soon as a woman becomes a mother, she learns to love and take responsibility for her child. But children also need to learn responsibility towards their parents. I have only one daughter. I give her all the love, but I also teach her that she must take care of me in my old age. Some children, unfortunately, don't realize this and end up hurting their parents. But if we instill this awareness in them from childhood, old age will never be difficult for anyone. If we educate them properly, old age will be a happy phase.

Srilatha: Absolutely, absolutely.

Jayaprakash: She is sharing her personal experience. The awareness we instill in children is crucial. Because one day, they too will become parents.

Srilatha: That's right.

Jayaprakash: And if they don't understand this, their children might treat them the same way. Isn't it important to be aware of this?

Srilatha: Think about the ocean. Just like it hides pearls and treasures within, a mother's love holds many life values. If a mother teaches these values when her children are young, through stories of great mothers and sons, children will naturally want to follow those ideals. Mothers should instill these values from childhood.

Jayaprakash: One special thing about mothers is that they accept their children as they are.

Srilatha: Absolutely.

Jayaprakash: There's a saying: *To a mother, even a limping child is precious.*

Srilatha: Even a limping child is precious.

Jayaprakash: No matter how the child is...

Srilatha: The mother loves them unconditionally.

Jayaprakash: Some kids make a mess, behave in all sorts of ways...

But to a mother, it doesn't matter.

Srilatha: Absolutely.

Jayaprakash: Isn't that right?

Srilatha: Certainly. This reminds me of a story. Once, Emperor Akbar said, *My son is the most beautiful of all.* To prove a point, Birbal took him to a hut where a mother was playing with her child. Even though the child wasn't conventionally beautiful, the mother was loving and playing with him as if he were the most precious being in the world. Seeing this, Akbar realized that to every mother, her child is the most beautiful. If we apply this lesson to our lives and accept people as they are, many of the social issues we face today could be reduced.

Jayaprakash: You explained that beautifully. Vishwanath Hande from Kundapura is calling. Vishwanath, Namaste.

Vishwanath: Namaste, sir. My question is, for a child's development, is parental guidance enough, or does the environment also play a role?

Jayaprakash: That's a very crucial question, Vishwanath. From your voice, I can tell you are experienced and wise. In a child's early years, parents play a major role. Later, teachers and society influence them. As Dr. Abdul Kalam mentioned, society plays a big role in shaping a child's personality. What do you think?

Srilatha: Definitely. Research shows that a child's development is influenced by genetics, but society also has a major impact. They learn from friends, teachers, parents, and relatives. In high school, they listen more to their friends and teachers than to their parents. All these factors shape their personality.

Jayaprakash: Definitely right. There is a call from Pune. Venkatesh is calling.

Venkatesh: Namaste. Wishing you a happy Gauri-Ganesha festival, Sir. In this era of modernization, every family usually has one or two children. During this time, the daughters-in-law who come to the house or the mothers who are already there—both should have motherly love towards each other. But in reality, this love and affection seem to be lacking. Instead, there is a kind of division—"this is mine, that is yours." Because of this, relationships are becoming strained, and a sort of friction starts.

This has become a common issue in every household nowadays. Either there is a lack of affection from the mother-in-law towards the daughter-in-law, or vice versa.

Jayaprakash: So, if you feel that love and care are lacking somewhere, society and all of us must become aware of this. We need to ensure that motherly affection exists even in the mother-in-law. Isn't that what we all want? What do you think?

Srilatha: Absolutely. When a daughter leaves her parents' home and comes to her husband's house, if the mother-in-law shows the same motherly love, there won't be conflicts. As we say in life:

*"Even though we are close, we remain distant,
trapped in our egos.*

Finding harmony in this short life is so difficult."

If both the mother-in-law and the daughter-in-law stop focusing on their egos and instead embrace the feeling of "our family," these problems would not arise.

Jayaprakash: Yes. When we look at the history of India's independence, we must remember Bhagat Singh and his mother, Vidyawati.

Srilatha: Definitely, sir. Today, we must remember Bhagat Singh. When he was about to be hanged, he told his mother, "Mother, don't cry. If you cry, even I will tear up." His mother replied, "No, my son, I am not crying. Everyone has to die one day, but I am proud that my son is sacrificing his life for the nation's freedom. Just shout 'Inquilab Zindabad' one last time before you go." Even in the moment of parting with her son, she displayed her patriotism alongside her motherly love. Similarly, today, we live safely because of our soldiers. They protect our nation.

Jayaprakash: Yes. Many mothers have sent their sons to serve the country.

Srilatha: We should bow to these brave mothers on this occasion.

Jayaprakash: Yes, especially when sending their sons into the army, these mothers support, encourage, and motivate their children.

Srilatha: Definitely.

Jayaprakash: That is very important, isn't it?

Srilatha: Absolutely. Because if you want your children to dedicate themselves to the nation, you must nurture patriotism in them from childhood. If a mother keeps her son only in her protective embrace and doesn't encourage him to explore beyond, it won't be possible. That's why a mother's role in inspiring children is crucial.

Jayaprakash: Even a genius like Thomas Alva Edison emerged because of his mother. Isn't that a historical fact?

Srilatha: Yes, sir. In today's society, if a child doesn't perform well in school, parents immediately scold them, asking, "Why didn't you do well? Why are your marks low?" But when Edison's teacher gave him a letter and he asked his mother what was written in it, his mother said, "Son, you are a genius. Your intelligence is far greater than what this school can handle. They have asked me to teach you myself." His mother became his teacher. Later in life, Edison found the same letter, which actually said, "Your son is mentally ill. We can no longer allow him in school." His mother had turned a negative into a positive, which shaped Edison into the great inventor he became.

Jayaprakash: Such incidents are truly inspiring. Anand is calling from Malur. Anand, namaste.

Anand: My question is, all the examples you are giving are from past generations. Nowadays, mothers focus only on their children's education. They don't encourage them to explore their interests or think about the country or society. Children are being confined only to academics. We don't see such mothers anymore.

Jayaprakash: Anand, our concern is the same. We share these examples so that today's parents can reflect on them. If they take inspiration from these mothers, they will think about how to raise their children holistically. We are emphasizing awareness. What do you think?

Srilatha: Absolutely. Today, another issue is that children have natural talents, but mothers often impose their own dreams on them. "Be an engineer, be a doctor"—instead of recognizing their child's natural abilities. If parents identify and encourage their children's true talents, it would be beneficial for both the child and society.

Jayaprakash: Yes. A mother always has a vision for her child. But some may lack educational awareness or role models to guide them. However, today's mothers should also inspire their children. It's not that they aren't doing it, but we should encourage more of it.

"Heaven must be really small because I can see it in my mom's eyes." A mother sees her entire world in her children, doesn't she?

Srilatha: Yes. Just as a mother sees heaven in her children, children should also see heaven in their mother's eyes.

Jayaprakash: Exactly. So, a mother is the root inspiration for a child's personality development, right?

Srilatha: Absolutely, sir.

Jayaprakash: Please share your thoughts.

Srilatha: As I mentioned earlier, schools today focus only on academic scores. But for a child's overall development, body, mind, intellect, and soul must be nurtured equally. Mothers should teach life values from the beginning, not just focus on marks.

Jayaprakash: There is a call from Udupi. Hello, namaste.

Srikari: Hello, namaste. Wishing you both a happy Gauri-Ganesha festival. I am Srikari from Udupi.

Jayaprakash: Please ask your question.

Srikari: No matter how far we are—whether abroad or in India— our first instinct when facing difficulties is to call our mother. When we talk to her, we feel at ease. Isn't that because of a mother's love?

Jayaprakash: Definitely. No matter the distance, the emotional bond with our mother remains strong. Even if someone in Bangalore is just a few kilometers away from their mother and only visits once a year, it is no different from someone in America doing the same. The connection is beyond physical distance. What do you think?

Srilatha: Absolutely. A mother is always close to our hearts. But another issue today is that while children grow up with their mother's love, as they become teenagers, they start feeling that their parents don't understand them. At the same time, parents feel that their children don't listen to them. If a mother truly understands her child's feelings, the child will always trust her, no matter what.

Jayaprakash: That is a great point, Srilatha. It's important not just to focus on academic performance but also on overall personality development.

Srilatha: Yes, sir. If we put cashews in a chili powder container and label it as cashews, will we ever find cashews inside? Similarly, if we force children into predefined career paths instead of recognizing their true potential, we won't allow their real talents to flourish. Instead, we should nurture their individuality and expose them to inspiring biographies.

Jayaprakash: Yes. We got a call from Huchegowda in Vasanthapura. Gowdru, namaste.

Huchegowda: Namaste, sir. My question is, a mother is like nature itself. Just as nature is the foundation of life, a mother is the foundation of all beings. When nature becomes angry, there is destruction. Similarly, when a mother is upset, children face the consequences. What do you think?

Jayaprakash: That's a wonderful thought! We must never take our mother's love for granted.

Srilatha: It is the children's responsibility to ensure their mother never reaches that point.

Shrilatha: Absolutely, sir.

Jayaprakash: When we talk about festivals, especially Ganesh Chaturthi, I felt like sharing a message related to a mother's love. You see, Lord Ganesha symbolizes many things. His large head represents "thinking big"—having grand ideas.

Shrilatha: A broad mind, a vast perspective...

Jayaprakash: Yes! His big ears signify listening more. His trunk teaches us to utilize opportunities wisely. His large belly symbolizes the ability to digest everything—be it food or life's joys and sorrows. In the same way, if we take the concept of a mother's love and apply it universally, wouldn't that help us embrace this perspective on a larger scale?

Shrilatha: Definitely, sir. Even when we look at Lord Ganesha, we see a mouse at his feet. The mouse is a very restless creature, yet Ganesha made it his vehicle. This teaches us that we too must control our restless minds. Similarly, if we nurture motherly love in every heart, we can bridge the gaps we see in today's world, where people often say there is no harmony. Every heart carries a mother's love—it is just a matter of having the eyes to see it.

Jayaprakash: True. Zig Ziglar once said, "Children go where there is excitement, but they stay where there is love." That's why some children start seeing their teachers as a second mother.

When they feel a lack of love from their mother, they often seek it elsewhere—even from their teachers. Isn't that so?

Shrilatha: Absolutely.

Jayaprakash: So, anyone working with children—whether in teaching or childcare—should embody a mother's love. We should, in a way, "inject" that motherly affection into them, right?

Shrilatha: Yes. Every child longs for a mother's love. When parents leave their kids in daycare, if the caretakers there show genuine affection, it's like an oasis in the desert for that child.

Jayaprakash: Exactly. Children crave warmth and affection. They long for love, don't they?

Shrilatha: Correct. Research even shows that emotional and creative development in children is deeply influenced by a mother's love. They say, *"A mother understands what a child does not say."* So, just as a mother understands an infant's unsaid emotions, she must also nurture and respond to the feelings of her child as they grow.

Jayaprakash: Yes. Shrilatha, how would you sum up your thoughts on a mother's love?

Shrilatha: A poem comes to mind:

> ***"Why search for God in stone and soil,***
> ***When does love and friendship dwell within us?"***

This means that love is already within us—we just need to recognize it. If every home fosters a mother's love, then the peace we all seek in life today will naturally follow. That is my wish: that every mother becomes an ideal mother.

Jayaprakash: Shrilatha, on this occasion of the Gauri-Ganesha festival, we have reflected on a mother's love. Let us pray that this motherly compassion grows in every heart and household. With that, we conclude today's discussion. Namaste to all.

Shrilatha: Namaste.

6.

Spiritual Mirror

A spiritual personality relates to the inner world of a human being and signifies the ability to transform different aspects of life, including economic, social, and personal elements. It involves understanding one's spiritual beliefs, thoughts, and purpose in life.

A spiritual personality consists of the following aspects:

1. Self-awareness: Understanding one's true nature.
2. Spiritual Practices: Methods such as meditation, prayer, or chanting that help purify the mind and soul.
3. Social Responsibility: A commitment to the welfare of others.
4. Spiritual Growth: Development of one's character through self-discipline, love, and compassion.

These elements shape a person's spiritual personality and help in the quest for the deeper meaning of life.

ಆಧ್ಯಾತ್ಮಿಕ
ಜೀವನ

Ways to Cultivate a Spiritual Personality

1. Meditation and Devotion: Set aside time daily for meditation, which helps calm the mind and enhance self-awareness.
2. Self-reflection: Regular introspection through journaling or observation to understand your emotions and beliefs.
3. Spiritual Literature: Reading teachings, scriptures, or spiritual books that provide new perspectives.
4. Positive Thinking: Replacing negative thoughts with optimistic and inspiring ones.
5. Service and Charity: Engaging in voluntary activities or community service to experience inner purification.
6. Heartfelt Compassion: Expressing love and kindness towards others to bring inner peace and happiness.
7. Faith and Devotion: Being sincere in your beliefs and incorporating them into daily life.
8. Healthy Relationships: Building meaningful relationships and surrounding yourself with spiritually inclined individuals.

Following these practices can enhance spiritual personality. However, every individual has their unique path; it is essential to consider personal experiences and needs.

Teachings from Spiritual Leaders on Spiritual Personality

Many great thinkers and spiritual leaders have emphasized the importance of spiritual personality and self-realization. Their teachings guide individuals toward understanding life's deeper essence.

1. **Mahatma Gandhi:**
   - "Spirituality is the core of my life. All my actions are based on spirituality. Morality is an inseparable part of spirituality."
2. **Swami Vivekananda:**
   - "No matter how successful you are in worldly life, without spiritual character, your life will never be complete."
3. **Jiddu Krishnamurti:**
   - "Spirituality is living without causing any form of suffering to others, living with love and peace."
4. **Dattatreya:**
   - "The essence of spirituality is self-realization. A true spiritual person must realize the divinity within himself."
5. **Rabindranath Tagore:**
   - "Spirituality is the flow of liberation; it frees you from the bonds of your emotions and fears."

6. **Mother Teresa:**
   - "Spirituality arises through sacrifice, charity, and compassionate service to others."

These teachings illuminate the significance of spiritual personality and serve as a guide for internal transformation and self-inquiry.

Spiritual Poetry on Self-Realization

Poetry has often been used to express deep spiritual insights, self-awareness, love, peace, and the truth of the soul. Some spiritual poems emphasize these aspects:

1. **Swami Vivekananda – "Self-Elevation"**

"Rise and awaken,
Your soul is a divine pilgrimage.
Seek the unexplored path,
To witness the divinity within you.
Everything may fade away,
But the light of your soul,
Will never diminish,
It is your true essence."

2. **Basavanna – "Kudala Sangama Deva"**

"I set out to become you,
I saw you as myself,
O Lord of Kudala Sangama,
In the lotus of your heart,
I found my own being,
Your vision is my true liberation."

3. **Raghavendra Swami – "Self-Realization"**

"This world appears real,
Only as long as we perceive it,
But the ultimate wisdom,
Lies in self-awareness.
The inner light guides us,
Towards the path of truth,
To merge with it completely,
Is to understand life's true meaning."

4. **Kanakadasa – "Surrender to You"**

"I see you within my soul,
Your divine form blesses my heart,
I surrender to you,
My sins dissolve in your grace.
With devotion, chants, and penance,
My soul's doors opened,
You and I are one,
This is the path of spirituality."

These poems inspire introspection, self-awareness, and a journey toward spiritual growth.

Famous Spiritual Masters and Their Teachings

Many spiritual masters have guided humanity toward self-realization and enlightenment. Some of the most influential figures include:

1. Gautama Buddha (563 BCE – 483 BCE)
   - The founder of Buddhism, Buddha's teachings focus on peace, compassion, and the middle path. He emphasized self-awareness, Nirvana, and liberation from suffering.
2. Jesus Christ (4 BCE – 30/33 CE)
   - The founder of Christianity, Jesus preached love, forgiveness, and peace. His teachings have profoundly influenced spiritual thought worldwide.
3. Swami Vivekananda (1863–1902)
   - A disciple of Ramakrishna Paramahamsa, he spread Indian Vedanta and spirituality worldwide.

His message, *"Arise, awake, and stop not till the goal is reached,"* is globally admired.

4. Dalai Lama (1935–Present)
   - The spiritual leader of Tibetan Buddhism, he advocates peace, tolerance, and spirituality as a way of life. His teachings emphasize universal compassion and inner peace.
5. Paramahansa Yogananda (1893–1952)
   - Introduced Kriya Yoga and meditation to the West. His book *"Autobiography of a Yogi"* is one of the most renowned spiritual texts globally.
6. Osho (Rajneesh) (1931–1990)
   - Osho's spiritual philosophy promotes the complete acceptance and experience of life, encouraging individuals to explore the depths of the human mind and soul.
7. Maharishi Mahesh Yogi (1918–2008)
   - Founder of Transcendental Meditation (TM), his teachings emphasize achieving mental balance and physical well-being through meditation.
8. Ramana Maharshi (1879–1950)
   - Known for his teachings on *Atma Vichara* (Self-inquiry), he guided seekers toward self-realization and spiritual enlightenment.

These spiritual masters have significantly influenced human consciousness, guiding individuals toward peace, self-awareness, and spiritual evolution.

How to Develop a Spiritual Life?

To be recognized as a spiritual being, one must align their lifestyle with inner peace, wisdom, and self-realization:

1. Meditation and Contemplation
2. Non-violence and Compassion
3. Simple Living and Humility
4. Self-Reflection and Awareness
5. Service to Others
6. Following Spiritual Principles
7. Unwavering Faith and Devotion
8. Ethics and Integrity
9. Seeing Divinity in Everyone
10. Wisdom and Detachment

By following these principles, one can cultivate a fulfilling spiritual life, leading to peace, enlightenment, and universal love.

A Spiritual Person and Their Influence on Life

A spiritual person leads their life with peace, kindness, and compassion, serving as a guiding light for others.

There is a deep connection between spirituality and personality because spirituality significantly impacts a person's inner growth and character. This relationship can be explained through the following aspects:

1. Self-discipline and Morality – Staying true to values and ethics.
2. Self-control – Developing patience and restraint.
3. Regulation of Thoughts and Emotions – Cultivating a balanced mindset.
4. Control Over Ego and Selfishness – Letting go of arrogance and self-centeredness.
5. Positive Thinking and Strong Willpower – Fostering optimism and resilience.

6. Inner Peace and Equilibrium – Maintaining mental and emotional stability.
7. Life's Purpose and Ideals – Understanding and following a meaningful path.
8. Love and Compassion for All – Treating others with empathy and kindness.

Spirituality awakens inner consciousness, strengthens mental resilience, and paves the way for a peaceful life. It serves as the inner force that inspires character, while personality acts as the means of applying spirituality in a social and practical manner.

We should embrace the belief: "Sarve Janah Sukhino Bhavantu" (May all beings be happy). We must adopt the mindset of "Vasudhaiva Kutumbakam" (The world is one family). Recognizing negativity is essential, but practicing positivity is even more important. We should strive to be good, perform noble actions, and embody humanity. True spirituality lies in understanding ourselves deeply and clearly.

Limitations

"I traveled by train,
Yet never saw the driver
Who controlled the engine from afar.

I flew in an airplane,
But never caught sight
Of the pilot steering the sky.

So, in this vast universe,
Can we truly see its driver?
He remains unseen,

His actions are his own,
And my journey is mine to take."

\- Jarganahalli Shivashankar

This poem beautifully captures the mystery of the unseen divine force that guides the universe, reminding us that while we may not always perceive the divine, we must continue our personal journey with faith and purpose.

6A.

Spirituality

An interview with Guru Bhagavan (Brahmarshi Gangadhar)

Jayaprakash Nagathihalli: Namaskara, good morning. A warm welcome to the "Chandada Chandanada Andada Belagu" program. Dear viewers, many elders say that a person's character becomes complete through spirituality. Those who immerse themselves in spirituality attain mental treasures like pearls and gems.

Today, our guest for the morning program is Brahmarshi Gangadhar, who served as an engineer for thirty years and has dedicated the last thirty years to the spiritual path. He has been actively involved in the renovation of ancient temples, religious service activities, and as a leader in various social service organizations.

Gangadhar has authored books such as *Modalu Maanavanagu, Parabrahma Vijnana, Chaitanya Pooje,* and *Jeevana Vijnana.* Many of his articles have also been published. He has expertise in spiritual disciplines such as *Sri Vidya Upasana, Reiki Grand Mastery, Atomic Healing,* and *Spiritual Healing.* Through the Chaitanya Healing Center, he provides training and free treatments.

Through his spiritual organization Parabrahma, he initiates seekers into *Parabrahma Diksha* and teaches the science of *Parabrahma.* In recognition of his selfless service, several organizations have honored him, and he has received the Seva Ratna Award.

Brahmarshi Gangadhar, a heartfelt welcome to our morning program. Namaskara!

Introduction & Personal Journey

Brahmarshi Gangadhar: Namaskara. *Om Guru Sakshat Parabrahma Tasmai Shri Gurave Namah. Om Shreem Hreem Parabrahmane Namah.*

Jayaprakash Nagatihalli: Brahmarshi Gangadhar, could you please introduce yourself, your hometown, and your spiritual mentors?

Brahmarshi Gangadhar: My ancestors were from Hosur, Gauribidanur Taluk. My grandfather lived there, but later, my father moved to Yelahanka. He worked as a primary school teacher in Yelahanka for about 25 years. I spent most of my life there and completed my college education.

By the time I was about 24-25 years old, I had lost both my parents. We had a joint family with my uncles, aunts, and cousins supporting me. After that, I took on family responsibilities. When I started working, my parents were no longer with me. I had to take care of my younger siblings and lead the household.

From a young age, I developed an interest in spirituality. There was a spiritual master, Shivananda Swami, in Yelahanka, whose guidance influenced me. My interest in spirituality grew over time, and I continued my journey alongside my professional and family responsibilities.

Later, I got married. My wife, Smt. J.K. Ramadevi has been my pillar of support in all my activities and service work. I consider myself fortunate in this regard. Whatever knowledge I have acquired, I have also shared with her.

Impact of Spirituality on Personality

Jayaprakash: Many believe that when one is drawn to spirituality, their personality transforms. What are your thoughts on this?

Brahmarshi Gangadhar: Absolutely! Human beings are inherently spiritual by nature, but we fail to recognize it. We consider ourselves separate from nature, which is the root cause of all problems. But in reality, nature itself brings spirituality within us.

If we analyze human existence, it comprises body, mind, soul, life force, and consciousness. If any of these is absent, human existence ceases to be. The foundation of all these elements is our spiritual essence. That is why we are born as spiritual beings in human embodiment.

The Creation of the Universe

Jayaprakash Nagathihalli: You are explaining this in a profound way. Do you believe that the universe was created in this manner?

Brahmarshi Gangadhar: Yes! According to the Vedas and Upanishads, before the universe was created, there existed a divine luminous point known as *Jyotirbindu*, which is also referred to as *Hiranyagarbha*. This primordial consciousness contained life force, knowledge, and energy.

Within this consciousness, there were three fundamental powers:

1. Ichha Shakti (Willpower)
2. Jnana Shakti (Knowledge Power)
3. Kriya Shakti (Action Power)

Due to the desire for creation, a resolution (Sankalpa) arose within the Jyotirbindu, leading to the formation of the universe. Scientific theories, like the Big Bang Theory, align with this concept.

The Jyotirbindu contained consciousness, energy, and vibrations. These led to contraction and expansion, which resulted in the formation of centrifugal and centripetal forces. This, in turn, generated wave movements, velocity, and acceleration, leading to the creation of the five fundamental elements (Panchabhutas)—earth, water, fire, air, and space.

At the subtle (sukshma) level and gross (sthula) level, nature manifested. The Vedic sages and Rishis recognized this primordial existence as Parabrahma, the supreme, all-knowing, all-powerful, and omnipresent force.

If we examine the universe (macrocosm) and human beings (microcosm), we find similarities:

- Universal energy exists in the cosmos, while human energy exists within us.
- Universal consciousness is mirrored in human consciousness.
- Universal mind and human mind function similarly.

In essence, just as the universe operates through Ichha (Will), Jnana (Knowledge), and Kriya (Action), the same principles exist within every human cell.

Human Existence and DNA Structure

Jayaprakash: That was a fascinating explanation of creation. Now, let's talk about human existence.

Brahmarshi Gangadhar: Human existence is a combination of body, mind, soul, life force, and consciousness. When we consider the physical body, it is made up of 46 chromosomes—23 inherited from the father and 23 from the mother.

On the first day of conception, a single-cell organism is formed in the mother's womb, known as the original cell. This DNA structure carries the blueprint of our existence. It governs everything from genetics to consciousness.

Jayaprakash: Yes, absolutely.

This conversation beautifully merges science and spirituality, explaining how the universe and human existence are interconnected. It emphasizes the idea that human beings are inherently spiritual and that understanding our spiritual essence helps us realign with nature and live a balanced life.

Brahmarshi Gangadhar: A single original cell divides into two, four, eight, sixteen, thirty-two, forty-eight genes, and our entire body develops in the mother's womb for nine months. After that, we are born. This is the truth of creation. In this process, the original cell contains a blueprint of our body—our structural blueprint—which is embedded by the Supreme Being. According to this blueprint, our body is formed.

Today, the DNA structure is so incredible that by analyzing DNA, we can determine our entire genetic history. It reveals our skin structure, hair type, height, qualities, flaws, ancestral lineage— including details about our parents, grandparents, uncles, and aunts. It can even predict details about our children. Moreover, if no natural calamities cause harm, it can estimate how long we might live. Such a marvelous structure has been created by the Supreme Being.

One more thing about DNA is that the entire creation—what is described in the Vedas as *Vasudhaiva Kutumbakam* (the world is one family)—is interconnected through DNA. If we examine the DNA structure of all living beings, we find that 40% of it is the same across all species. The remaining 60% varies through different permutations and combinations, leading to the diverse forms of life in creation.

Jayaprakash Nagathihalli: There is the physical body that we see, but there is also a subtle body, an aura around a person. Can you provide some information on this?

Brahmarshi Gangadhar: Yes, that is true. What we see is the *gross body*, which medical science describes as being made up of blood, flesh, bones, skin, nerves, and cells. However, modern science also acknowledges that every animate and inanimate object has an *energy field*, which is scientifically called the *electromagnetic field*. In ancient times, sages and seers referred to this as the *prabha valaya* (aura) or the *subtle body.*

Jayaprakash: This *prabha valaya* (aura) contains *pancha koshas* (five sheaths) and *chakras*, right? Can you elaborate on that?

Brahmarshi Gangadhar: Yes. Within our gross body, there is a *central axis*, and surrounding it, extending up to about three feet, is our subtle body. This subtle body consists of seven layers, each with its own physical characteristics, mental attributes, vibration patterns, and frequency.

Then there are *chakras*, which are classified as major, minor, and mini chakras. Since the head, torso, hands, and legs contain major organs, the chakras in these regions are called *major chakras.* Ancient sages identified five sheaths—*annamaya kosha* (food sheath), *pranamaya kosha* (life energy sheath), *manomaya kosha* (mental sheath), *vijnanamaya kosha* (intellect sheath), and *anandamaya kosha* (bliss sheath). The chakras are named *Muladhara* (root), *Swadhisthana* (sacral),

Manipura (solar plexus), *Anahata* (heart), *Vishuddha* (throat), *Ajna* (third eye), and *Sahasrara* (crown).

These chakras are marvelously designed by the Supreme Being. What do they do? In ancient times, sages performed deep meditation for years, without modern conveniences like drinking coffee in the morning or eating meals in the afternoon. How did they survive? They understood the technology of the subtle body. By activating these chakras, they aligned with the *Universal Life Force*.

Each chakra acts as both a *receiver* and a *transmitter* of this energy. Just as a police inspector oversees law and order in a specific area, each chakra regulates the corresponding organs, nervous system, cells, and endocrine glands. When chakras function properly, diseases automatically disappear.

Sages and enlightened beings could see this aura. Even today, there are people in Bangalore who can see it. In 1939, a Russian scientist named *Semyon Kirlian* discovered a special type of photography called *Kirlian photography*, which captured the subtle body's image. He even won a *Nobel Prize* for this discovery.

Jayaprakash: So, with this technique, we can see a person's subtle body?

Brahmarshi Gangadhar: Absolutely! Not just humans, but all living beings.

Jayaprakash: All living beings?

Brahmarshi Gangadhar: Yes. Even a leaf has a subtle body. Scientists in America conducted multi-million-dollar research experiments titled *The Secret Life of Plants*, demonstrating that when a leaf is plucked, it experiences pain, and its subtle energy field reacts and changes color. Such scientific findings confirm the existence of subtle energy.

Jayaprakash: You have explained the subtle body beautifully. Now, let's talk about the *mind*. The human mind is fascinating. Can you share some insights into its nature and functioning?

Brahmarshi Gangadhar: Certainly. *Man eva manushyanam karanam bandha mokshayoh*—the mind is the cause of both bondage and liberation.

But what exactly is the *mind*? The mind has no color, no smell, no shape, no weight—yet it exists. What is it then? It is just a *state of being*.

Jayaprakash: Does it exist as we perceive it?

Brahmarshi Gangadhar: Yes! It is a *bundle of thoughts*. Without thoughts, there is no mind. The mind depends entirely on the five senses (*panchendriyas*). If the senses do not function, the mind loses its existence.

For example, imagine a blind grandfather asking his grandson what he is drinking. The child says, "Milk." The grandfather asks, "What is milk like?" The child replies, "It is white." The grandfather then asks, "What is white?" The child, trying to explain, points to a crane and says, "White like that bird." But since the grandfather has never seen a crane, he cannot understand. This proves that without sensory perception, the mind cannot grasp reality.

The mind, which has no real substance, dictates our lives like a *dictator*. The body has only basic needs, but the mind uses the body as a tool to fulfill its desires.

Jayaprakash: You have explained the mind beautifully. Now, can you talk about the *spiritual existence* of humans?

Brahmarshi Gangadhar: Certainly! *Spirituality* is the *science of the spirit*.

Many confuse *spirituality* with *religion*. Religion is like a *river*—it has boundaries. Each religion is like a different river, such as the *Ganga, Kaveri, or Yamuna*. However, spirituality is like the *sky*—infinite and without boundaries.

The Earth exists within the sky, and we exist on Earth, meaning we are also tiny sources of energy in this vast universe. As humans, we are born as *spiritual beings* in a physical body. Every living cell contains divine energy.

One key element in this is *love*. The Supreme Being has instilled love in every being—hatred does not originate from the divine. This divine spiritual existence is what makes us who we are.

Jayaprakash: What about *prana* (life force)? We say, "His life force has departed." What exactly is *prana*?

Brahmarshi Gangadhar: *Prana* is the *subtlest of the subtle energies*, often equated with *consciousness* (*chaitanya*). It is a deeply profound subject, but in short, it is the vital force that sustains life.

Jayaprakash: And *consciousness*? We talk about different types of consciousness—social consciousness, general awareness, etc. What is *consciousness*?

Brahmarshi Gangadhar: Consciousness is an extremely subtle existence. It belongs to the level of the *soul*, whereas the *mind* belongs to the physical level. However, consciousness exists in every living cell.

When I explained DNA earlier, I mentioned that *consciousness* is present in every cell. But beyond this, there is also *willpower, knowledge, and divine energy...*

Jayaprakash: Tell me.

Brahmarshi Gangadhar: Look at this. This is an electric bulb. If you understand this, it is like understanding our entire life.

Jayaprakash: Please explain.

Brahmarshi Gangadhar: See, an electric bulb has a connector, a glass tube in the middle, a filament, and an outer and inner layer. This is its structure. When current passes through it, light is emitted from the center. If it is a 100-watt bulb, it lights up the room with 100-watt intensity. If it is 1,000 watts, it emits 1,000-watt brightness.

Jayaprakash: Yes.

Brahmarshi Gangadhar: Now, what happens if dust accumulates on the outer or inner layer? The light diminishes.

Jayaprakash: Yes, the brightness reduces.

Brahmarshi Gangadhar: Exactly. The core brightness does not reduce, but due to the dust, it appears dim. If we clean the dust, the light shines fully without any obstruction. Our life is just as subtle. This bulb is an example of Brahma Vidya (spiritual knowledge).

This is our body. The outer layer is our physical body. The inner layer is our mind. The filament in the middle represents our soul. When awareness (electricity) flows, the Atma Jyoti (light of the soul) glows. From the time we are in the womb until our last breath, the Atma Jyoti is always shining. But when impurities accumulate in our body and mind, we fail to realize its presence. How can we then recognize it in others?

That is why, just as we cleanse our bodies daily through bathing, we must also meditate to cleanse our minds. When we remove mental impurities through meditation, inner and outer purification occurs, and we realize the brilliance of our soul.

Jayaprakash: With just a simple example of a bulb, you have explained the entire concept of spirituality, Brahmarshi. Now, regarding sound therapy, you say it has unique healing properties. Can you explain?

Brahmarshi Gangadhar: Of course. Sound is truly marvelous. There is Anahata Nada (unstruck sound) and also worldly sounds. Let me demonstrate. Look at this Tibetan bell. It has no tongue, yet it produces the sound of "Om." Humans, even with a tongue, hesitate before uttering "Om." Listen, I will show you.

Using this Tibetan bell in your home, if you strike it 33 times every morning and evening, it corrects Vastu doshas (architectural imbalances) and harmonizes the energy in your home. This bell is made of seven metals and has a special power.

Now, look at these singing bowls. They are also made of seven metals. I use them for healing. When I first visited Nepal, I saw these instruments and learned about their effects. My yoga master, K.R. Srinivasa Murthy, inspired me to use them for therapy. These bowls emit vibrations that resonate as Om.

When you place these bowls on the body and strike them, they create sound waves. These waves bring deep relaxation by taking the mind into an alpha state of meditation. Additionally, the vibrations travel through every cell, nerves, organs, bones, and endocrine glands, rejuvenating the entire body. It balances the gross body, subtle body, mind, and chakras, bringing harmony. I have conducted many experiments and found that in just 10 minutes, this therapy can significantly heal ailments.

Jayaprakash: This sound wave therapy seems to resonate through the entire body!

Brahmarshi Gangadhar: Yes.

Jayaprakash: It creates a kind of vibration. What is the universal message about love and life?

Brahmarshi Gangadhar: Absolutely! Here is a wonderful message:

- LOVE stands for Living Organism Vibration Energy.
- Love is the essence of life.
- Love is crystal clear.
- Love is unconditional.

- Love is positive energy.
- Love is an eternal force.
- Love is God.

Similarly, LIFE also has a beautiful meaning:

- LIFE stands for Love Inherent Fundamental Energy.

And what about the SOUL?

- SOUL stands for Source of Universal Love.

My divine message is simple:

Have full faith in yourself, be faithful to yourself, be truthful to yourself, be sincere to yourself, be loving to yourself, be good and do good. Open your heart and see, God is within you and all around you.

Jayaprakash: That was such a profound universal message! What are the spiritual centers in the human body?

Brahmarshi Gangadhar: Yes. The Ajna Chakra (third eye center) corresponds to the pineal and pituitary glands. It is known as the center of wisdom, where the divine guru resides.

Then, at the thymus gland (one inch below the throat), we have the Ankaha Karana Kendra—the seat of the soul. This is where Paramatma (Supreme Soul) resides.

Next, at the navel (Manipura Chakra), we have the Antaranga Kendra—the seat of the Divine. This is why we call God Antaranga Vasi (the one residing within). So, Guru (wisdom), Atma (soul), and Deva (divine) are all within us. There is no need to search outside.

Another fascinating truth is about our chromosomes. We inherit 23 chromosomes from our father and 23 from our mother, forming our physical body. This means our body is a reflection of our parents. When we say "Matru Devo Bhava" (Mother is God) and "Pitru Devo Bhava" (Father is God), we are not only honoring them but also respecting our own body.

Who is the true guru of any person?

It is one's own soul—the innate, divine guide. All other teachers are worldly gurus. When we say "Gurubhyo Namah" or "Acharyabhyo Namah", we are saluting our teachers as well as our own inner self.

Jayaprakash: Brahmarshi Gangadhar, you have shared deep knowledge about the body, subtle body, mind, light, and aura. We are truly grateful for this wisdom. Namaste.

Brahmarshi Gangadhar: Namaste.

6B.

A Positive Attitude

Transcript of a Video

Jayaprakash

In our world, along with humans, there are also animals. Among them, we observe wild animals from a distance, which makes it difficult to understand their nature and behavior. However, wildlife photographers study them closely and introduce them to the general public. One such wildlife photographer is H. Satish, who has participated in global competitions and won over 400 international awards. Let's hear from him.

You have captured many animals up close. Your experience is immense. How can we better understand these animals?

H. Satish

First and foremost, to engage in wildlife photography, one must possess the ability and knowledge. Whether it is wildlife photography or understanding animals and birds, having basic knowledge is essential. If we consider photography as 100%, then 80% of it is about understanding wildlife behavior, and only 10% is about capturing the photograph.

Two years ago, in Bandipur, tourists used to stop their cars in the middle of the jungle road, get out, and take photos of elephants up close with automatic cameras. If an elephant is calm, it allows photos, but if it is in a musth state, it can be dangerous.

I have taken photos of wild elephants from just 10 feet away without any issues. However, if a tourist carelessly approaches with an automatic camera, incidents of elephants overturning vehicles have also been reported. This is not just about elephants but applies to tigers, leopards, and bears as well. Animals fear humans as much as humans fear them.

For instance, people panic upon seeing a snake, but snakes fear humans even more. In our childhood, we learned that forests have ferocious animals like tigers, leopards, and bears. But in reality, there are no cruel animals in the wild. If you want to see a cruel creature, look in the mirror—that is the only cruel being.

Every animal and bird in the forest is peaceful by nature. They attack only when they feel threatened or need to protect their young.

Elephants, for example, protect their calves by keeping them between adults, preventing any external threats.

Jayaprakash

Wildlife photography comes with risks. Capturing animals like elephants, tigers, and lions—what if they suddenly attack?

H. Satish

In wildlife photography, one must remain calm. In North India's Ranthambore Wildlife Sanctuary, famous for its tigers, I once encountered a tiger in a narrow valley with no way to escape. However, as long as I remained still and did not disturb it, the tiger simply walked past me within two feet.

At Bannerghatta National Park, tigers are shown to visitors through a van ride. About ten years ago, a man teasing a tiger ended up getting pulled away by it. Zoo animals behave differently from those in the wild.

People often ask, "What if a tiger or leopard eats you?" If that were to happen, I would be happy because, as a wildlife photographer, that would be the kind of death I would desire.

Mindset Towards Money

Jayaprakash

How we perceive money is crucial. Many people place immense value on wealth. However, we have seen poor people living happily, while some wealthy individuals, despite having large mansions, are unhappy.

Some people earn ₹1,000 a month, while others make crores. Does that mean only the rich can be happy? The key is not how much money we have but how we manage it and our attitude towards it.

For example, a man bought a Ferrari after working hard, but he soon realized how expensive it was to maintain. Friends started approaching him for benefits, strangers expected hefty tips, and parking attendants treated him differently. That's when he understood the importance of wisely managing his purchases.

Similarly, winning a ₹1 crore lottery doesn't ensure long-term wealth if one is not accustomed to handling large sums. Many lottery winners end up losing their money in just a few months because they lack the mindset to manage it properly.

Mindset Towards Time

Jayaprakash

Everyone must respect time. No matter where we are in the world, each person has only 24 hours in a day. I once wrote a short poem:

"Whether dark-skinned or fair-skinned,
Whether short or tall,

Nature has given us all
The same amount of time."

We often see framed photographs in people's homes with two dates inscribed—one being the date of birth and the other, the date of death. I call this the DOB-DOD concept.

We celebrate our birth date every year, but we don't know the other date. What we can do is focus on today and make the most of the time we have left. Instead of worrying about lost time, we should set goals and plan for the future.

A railway track is a great analogy. One track represents time that has already passed, while the other represents the journey ahead. We must move forward while staying on track. Some people say that managing time is like playing chess—you sometimes need to take calculated moves, retreat when necessary, or adapt to new challenges.

A person who values time also cultivates discipline. If we respect time, time will respect us in return, and we will find joy in our work.

Mindset Towards Service

Jayaprakash

Let's also reflect on the mindset towards service. We often hear that the more we give, the more we receive. Many wealthy people believe that generosity brings prosperity.

Not everyone has money to donate, but people can still serve in different ways. Some offer their time by volunteering for social causes. Others adopt orphaned children despite having their own.

This reminds me of Purandaradasa's words:

> *"Those who pour water back into the lake*
> *Will receive blessings in abundance."*

How much we contribute to society is in our hands, and I urge everyone to engage in service in whatever way they can.

M. Sadashiv, Tax Consultant, Sadashiv & Co.

From the beginning, I always wanted to serve society. I have gained so much from the community, and I always felt the need to give back. Coming from a poor background, I understood the importance of helping others.

One of my close friends, Assistant Commissioner Srinivas Murthy, introduced me to Krishna Trust, where they needed volunteers. Initially, I joined for three months, but eventually, I was asked to take on the role of President.

For the past eight years, I have been running a school for children with intellectual disabilities, treating them as my own. I believe that serving society is the greatest satisfaction one can have.

This passage discusses various perspectives on optimism, inclusivity, social responsibility, environmental consciousness, and personal growth through the voices of different individuals.

- **Uma Jayakumar,** a beauty expert, talks about her initiative to train and empower differently-abled individuals, whom she refers to as "silent warriors" instead of using traditional labels. She teaches them beauty skills, providing them with employment opportunities in her parlor, and emphasizes the importance of patience and understanding their language.

- **Ananth R. Koppar,** CEO of KTWO Technologies, shares how his middle-class upbringing influenced his views on financial responsibility. He and his wife decided to use their IT earnings for meaningful social causes. Inspired by corporate social responsibility, they encourage others in the industry to give back to society.
- **B.R. Nagesh,** an environmentalist, discusses the importance of protecting local lakes. He believes lakes should be treated as sacred and urges communities to prevent pollution by taking collective responsibility. He highlights how safeguarding water resources is essential for future generations.
- **Jayaprakash,** the speaker, emphasizes the power of perspective by narrating stories from mythology and everyday life. He shares a Mahabharata anecdote about Duryodhana and Dharmaraya, demonstrating how our mindset shapes our view of the world. Through simple analogies like a rose among thorns or a half-filled glass, he illustrates the difference between an optimist and a pessimist.

The overarching message is about fostering a positive mindset, embracing social responsibility, and viewing challenges as opportunities for growth and contribution.

7.

FINANCIAL MIRROR

Economic Personality refers to an individual's financial tendencies, money management skills, and decision-making related to finances. It is influenced by factors such as financial capability, income-expense management, investment habits, savings practices, and debt handling.

Economic personality plays a crucial role in determining a person's quality of life, financial security, and long-term economic success.

Several factors influence economic personality in different ways. Some key factors include:

1. Financial Status
2. Money Management
3. Financial Education
4. Perspective and Goals
5. Economic and Cultural Background
6. Financial Thinking

These factors shape an individual's personality and impact how they make financial decisions, structure their lives, and manage their resources.

ಆರ್ಥಿಕ
ಜೀವನ

Quotes on Economic Personality and Financial Ethics

Many well-known personalities have shared their perspectives on financial management and economic personality. Here are some significant quotes:

1. Warren Buffett:

    "Do not save what is left after spending, but spend what is left after saving."

    (Do not save what remains after spending; instead, spend what remains after saving.)

2. Benjamin Franklin:

    "Beware of little expenses; a small leak will sink a great ship."

    (Be mindful of small expenses; even a tiny leak can sink a big ship.)

3. Peter Drucker:

    "The best way to predict the future is to create it."

    (The best way to foresee the future is to shape it yourself.)
4. Robert Kiyosaki:

    "It's not how much money you make, but how much money you keep, how hard it works for you, and how many generations you keep it for."

(What matters is not how much money you earn, but how much you retain, how effectively it works for you, and how long it lasts across generations.)

5.   Tony Robbins:

"It's not about the amount of money you make, but the amount of money you retain and grow."

(It is not about how much money you earn, but how much you save and grow.)

6.   Adam Smith:

"All money is a matter of belief."

(Money is fundamentally a matter of trust.)

7.   Rich DeVos:

"Money cannot buy peace of mind. It cannot heal ruptured relationships or build meaning into a life that has none."
(Money cannot purchase mental peace, repair broken relationships, or provide meaning to an otherwise meaningless life.)

These insights emphasize that economic personality extends beyond financial management—it also connects with an individual's ethics, cultural influences, and long-term goals.

Ways to Enhance Economic Personality

Improving economic personality is essential for long-term financial success. Here are some effective strategies:

1. Financial Education:
   Read financial books, take online courses, and attend workshops to enhance your financial knowledge.
2. Budgeting:
   Create a budget to track your income and expenses. This helps in better expense management and increased savings.
3. Saving and Investing:
   Develop habits of saving and investing. Utilize savings accounts and structured investment plans for financial growth.
4. Setting Financial Goals:
   Define your financial objectives, whether it's buying a house, planning for retirement, or achieving short-term financial milestones.
5. Capital Management:
   Diversify investments and learn strategies for efficient capital management.
6. Discipline and Decision-Making:
   Practice patience and careful planning in financial decisions. Take time to analyze situations and make informed choices.
7. Financial Awareness:
   Before making purchases, critically assess their necessity and financial impact.
8. Creating Stable Income Sources:
   Focus on building sustainable income sources through investments, businesses, or other financial assets.

9. Adopting a Growth Mindset:
   Look for new ways to improve financial stability. Explore creative and strategic financial opportunities.
10. Seeking Financial Mentorship:
   Learn from financially successful individuals. Engage in discussions, follow good financial practices, and apply valuable insights.

By adopting these strategies, one can enhance their economic personality, leading to better financial management and long-term success.

Financial Management: Effective Ways to Use and Save Money

1. Creating a Budget:
   Record your income and expenses, and create a budget to keep your spending under control. Differentiate between essential and discretionary expenses.
2. Tracking Income and Expenses:
   Keep a daily or monthly record of your earnings and spending. This helps you understand your financial situation better.
3. Prioritizing Savings:
   Set financial goals and allocate a percentage of your income to a savings account.
4. Considering Investments:
   Instead of just saving, focus on investing as well. Have a well-planned investment strategy to grow your money.
5. Debt Management:
   Pay off all loans as soon as possible. Prioritize clearing high-interest debts first.

6. Avoiding Unnecessary Purchases:
    Think before you buy. Instead of making impulsive purchases, wait 24-72 hours before deciding.
7. Having a Financial Plan:
    Set long-term goals, including retirement and emergency funds, and plan investments accordingly.
8. Financial Education:
    Enhance your financial knowledge by reading books, attending online courses, and staying informed about financial matters.
9. Using Different Accounts:
    Explore various financial options that help manage money efficiently, earn better interest, or reduce expenses.
10. Consulting a Financial Advisor:
    If you lack experience in financial management, consider seeking advice from a financial expert.

By following these financial management tips, you can achieve financial stability and long-term success.

Steps to Become Wealthy

Those aspiring to become wealthy can follow some essential strategies. Here are some key tips:

1. Prioritizing Investments:
    Focus on investing, not just saving. Consider stock markets, capital funds, bonds, and other financial instruments.
2. Financial Education:
    Learn more about finance and money management. Read books and take online courses on financial literacy.

3. Starting Your Own Business:
    Consider launching your own business. This can help generate higher income and increase wealth.
4. Budgeting and Saving:
    Control your expenses by creating a budget. Save a percentage of your earnings and invest it wisely.
5. Setting Financial Goals:
    Have both long-term and short-term financial goals. Create a strategy to achieve them.
6. Managing Expenses Wisely:
    Reduce unnecessary expenses. Before making a new purchase, evaluate whether it is genuinely needed.
7. Generating Passive Income:
    Establish sources of passive income, such as rental properties, investments, or online sales.
8. Building Relationships and Networking:
    Connect with successful individuals in the financial sector. Expanding your network can help identify new opportunities.
9. Continuous Effort:
    Wealth-building is a long-term process. Work hard and keep exploring new opportunities.
10. Learning from Experts:
    Observe and learn from successful entrepreneurs and financial experts about how they accumulated wealth.

By following these principles, you can develop a wealth-building mindset and take necessary actions to achieve financial prosperity.

Quick Ways to Earn Money

Here are some professions and opportunities that allow for rapid income generation:

1. Freelancing:
   Jobs like content writing, graphic design, web development, and social media management can help earn money quickly.
2. Online Tutoring/Classes:
   If you are an expert in a subject, consider offering

7A.

Money Management

Success Secrets with Jayaprakash Nagathihalli

Anchor:
To give us more insights into money management, we have with us today an expert who will talk about how to view money, how to use it systematically, and all related details. Joining us today is personal development expert Jayaprakash Nagathihalli. A warm welcome to the program, sir. Let's start with the importance of money.

Jayaprakash:
If we don't have money, it feels like something is missing in life. Whatever work we do, money is essential. The reason we have chosen this topic today is that some people have a casual approach towards money. They lack sufficient understanding of financial matters or have small misconceptions in their perspective on money. We need to change our outlook on money.

Money is a medium. It helps us carry out transactions. It could be rupees in our country, dollars elsewhere, or any other currency. From the perspective of transactions, money is an integral part of our lives, and that is a fact.

Anchor:
People often say, "Money is power" or "Money is everything."
What does that mean, sir?

Jayaprakash:
Think about it—if we have a lot of money in our bank account, we
naturally feel more confident. Why does that happen? Because
when we have money, we can obtain most of the things we need
and access better services.

The more money we have, the higher our confidence and self-
assurance. This is why understanding money correctly is a crucial
success secret.

When people say "money is everything," they mean money has
the power to get things done. Many people take different paths to
earn money. Having money gives a certain power, and there's
nothing wrong with that. However, what matters is how we use it.
If we use money wisely and not wastefully, our perception of it
improves. Ultimately, money is just a medium of exchange. In
fact, there is even a Kannada movie titled *Dudde Doddappa*
(Money is Everything).

Anchor:
People say one should have *belief* in money. What does that
mean?

Jayaprakash:
Many people say, "I never seem to get money," or "My fate isn't
good," or "Money never stays in my hands." But if we stop
thinking negatively and start using money wisely, we will attract
it. There's no doubt about that—our destiny is shaped by our
mindset.

Instead of saying, "I can never earn money," ask yourself, "How much do I need? What are my desires?" Set a goal and work towards it in the right way. If you continuously put in the effort, you will achieve what you desire.

Having a positive attitude towards money is very important. Some people say they don't care about money, but deep down, they know its value. Sometimes, people who say they don't need money are the ones struggling without it.

Anchor:
How can we cultivate a *positive* attitude towards money?

Jayaprakash:
Money is not a bad thing. Some people believe money is evil, but that's incorrect. Money itself has no moral value—it is just a currency, a note, or a coin.

When we view money positively and respect it, we tend to attract more of it. Many people even pray for wealth, which is fine, but along with prayer, we must work hard.

Some people set small goals—earning thousands, while others set bigger goals—earning lakhs or even crores. Why do some people make crores while others struggle for thousands? It's because of their mindset and their targets. If someone sets a goal of earning ₹100 crores but falls short, they might still make ₹70 crores.

Our perception, understanding, and interactions with money are all crucial. Therefore, let's view money positively, think optimistically, and always speak about money in a constructive way. Let's avoid statements like "Money ruined my life" or

"Everything is destroyed because of money." If we change our mindset, we can attract financial success.

Anchor:
In this context, how can we use *mind power* effectively?

Jayaprakash:
We have been talking about positivity. *Mind power* is crucial. If someone wants to earn ₹100 crores, they need to develop a strategy and give their brain work to do.

There's a phrase I often use: "Mind your mind, and your mind will mind you." If you focus on your mind, your mind will focus on you. If you firmly decide to earn ₹100 crores, your mind will start working towards making it happen.

To do this, we must keep our minds calm, peaceful, and stress-free. Confidence grows when we believe in ourselves. *Self-belief* is very important. When we trust ourselves, self-awareness also increases. With greater self-awareness, our clarity improves, obstacles disappear, and the right path becomes visible.

Opportunities exist everywhere. For example, learning DTP (Desktop Publishing) can open up many part-time job options. Learning Tally can help someone get accounting work. Skills create income opportunities.

A person can even monetize hobbies. A photographer with limited time can collaborate with a studio on weekends and earn extra money. Over time, they might even start their own studio or business.

The key is to give the brain something to work on. When we do this, we start seeing more opportunities around us.

That's why *mind power* is crucial. We must constantly tell ourselves, "I can become rich."

Being wealthy is not just about numbers. Some people feel rich with just ₹10,000 in the bank, while others don't feel wealthy even with ₹10 crores.

So, ask yourself—what does being rich mean to *you*? How much money would make *you* happy? Set that amount as a goal and work towards it. Your mind will then start finding ways to achieve it.

There's a concept called the Law of Attraction. Many people around the world follow this theory. When you strongly desire something and take action towards it, you attract it into your life.

If we align our efforts with our desires, there's no doubt that everyone can become wealthier than they are today. That's the message I'd like to share.

7B.

STOCK MARKET

This is a detailed English translation of the conversation between **Dr. Bharat Chandra and Jayaprakash** about **stock market investments**:

Jayaprakash:

Dear friends, greetings! With me today is Dr. Bharat Chandra, a well-known name in Karnataka when it comes to the stock market. Through his institute, Dr. Bharat Chandra has been guiding many people online.

Sir, greetings! The stock market often raises many questions among common people. Nowadays, banks, post offices, and public provident funds are being heavily promoted. Despite that, why should one invest in the stock market? That is my first question.

Dr. Bharat Chandra:

That's an excellent question. The interest we get from banks, post offices, and provident funds is only about 6-8%. However, inflation also stands at 6-8%.

What does this mean? If you invest money in a post office today and withdraw it after five years or even one year, inflation will have increased the cost of essentials, such as rice, to the extent that the money you saved may not even be sufficient to buy the same quantity. Your money loses value every year due to inflation.

To secure your retirement and future financial needs, you *must* invest in the stock market or mutual funds. Even if you don't invest all your money, at least a small portion should be allocated to these. By doing so, you can expect returns of 13%, 15%, 18%, or even 20%. This will help you cover future expenses like your children's education, marriage, purchasing a home, and retirement.

If people don't *learn* about stock market investments or *practice* investing in them, they will *definitely* regret it in the future. This is something I say from experience.

Jayaprakash:

Sir, that sounded like a statutory warning—like a legal caution you just issued! Dr. Bharat Chandra, in life, we are given many choices and opportunities between birth and death. My curiosity is, when is the *right* time to start investing?

Dr. Bharat Chandra:

The moment you start getting money in your hands—perhaps when your parents give you pocket money—is the time you should start thinking about saving. Suppose your parents give you ₹5,000 as pocket money for bus fare and canteen expenses. Can you try to save at least ₹1,000 from that?

But *mandatory* investing should begin as soon as you get your first salary. I have observed many people, especially those in their 20s and 30s, who prioritize spending on their children's education and marriage first. Education is visible to them— enrolling their child in a good school, nursery, or engineering college. Then comes marriage, which also requires financial planning.

People often *neglect* retirement planning, realizing its importance only at 40-50 years of age. Remember, banks will *lend* you money for your child's education or marriage, but nobody will lend you money for retirement! After retirement, you won't have a salary to pay off EMIs.

So, from the *first* salary itself, you must aim to save *at least* 25-35% of your income.

If you are 25 years old, you may not have many expenses—your parents may still provide food, clothing, and shelter. That means you can save more. By 28, you may get married, by 30, you may have your first child, by 33, the second child, by 36, you may buy a car, and by 60, you will retire. By 65, hospital visits may start.

So, the key question is: How do you start saving today?

Jayaprakash:

Sir, that was very insightful and easy to understand. I've also heard people say, *"Don't put all your investments in one place. Diversify your investments."* Many people invest in real estate and gold. What percentage of our investment should go into stocks?

Dr. Bharat Chandra:

I can see that you are speaking from experience. Yes, you *shouldn't* put all your eggs in one basket. If a cat enters your home, it might eat all the eggs.

The right way to invest is as follows:

- If your total savings is ₹100,
    - Keep 10% in banks,
    - Invest 5% in gold,
    - Allocate 5% to insurance,
    - Invest 50% in real estate (because land and property prices in urban areas are very high),
    - The remaining 30% should go into the stock market.

Even in stock market investments, do not put all your money into just *one* company. Instead, diversify your 30% investment into at least 8-10 sectors and spread it across 8-10 different stocks.

If you invest all your money in *one* company, and someday the chairman of that company makes a bad decision, you will suffer the consequences.

Jayaprakash:

Sir, earlier, people believed that everyone in a mental hospital was mentally ill. But over time, that perception changed. Similarly, today, when someone invests in the stock market, many people say, *"You will definitely incur a loss."* What would you say about this as an expert in the field?

Dr. Bharat Chandra:

People wrongly equate stocks with losses.

There are over 2,000 stocks listed on the National Stock Exchange. Out of these:

- 200 stocks are profitable,
- 100 are neutral,
- 1,700-1,800 stocks are loss-making.

So, a stock market expert studies historical data and identifies companies that have consistently given good returns for 10-20 years.

A profitable company today is *likely* to continue being profitable in the future.

Jayaprakash:

That reminds me of old traditions! In arranged marriages, families didn't just look at the bride or groom; they investigated the family background—grandparents, financial status, and values. Isn't that similar to researching a company before investing?

Dr. Bharat Chandra:

Exactly! People used to ask, "What was the boy's salary five years ago? How much is it now? What might it be in the future?"

Similarly, in stock market investing, you should analyze:

- What was the company's profit 10 years ago?
- What was it 5 years ago?
- Is it consistently growing?

There are two types of analysis:

1. Fundamental Analysis – Examining financial statements, profit trends, assets, liabilities, and loan repayments.
2. Technical Analysis – Studying price movement graphs, moving averages, RSI (Relative Strength Index), and candlestick patterns.

Just like a general doctor uses a stethoscope and a cardiologist uses ECG to diagnose heart issues, fundamental analysis gives a broad picture, while technical analysis provides deeper insights.

Jayaprakash:

The most important question—how much profit can one expect from stock market investments?

Dr. Bharat Chandra:

Great question! We have researched this extensively.

For example, Titan Company has given an average return of 30% per year over the last 24 years (since 2000).

- A bank gives 8% returns.
- Titan gives 30% returns.
- That's 4 times more!

If you invest in a post office savings scheme, saving ₹10,000-₹20,000 per month, you may accumulate ₹60-70 lakhs by retirement.

But, if you invest the *same* amount in good stocks, you could retire with ₹20-30 crores!

A 25-year-old investing ₹5,000 per month in stocks with 20% returns could accumulate ₹21 crores by the age of 60!

Jayaprakash:

Sir, you have given us incredibly valuable insights! Thank you so much.

7C.

Earn Love, Respect, Relationships, and Experiences Along with Money

Jayaprakash Nagathihalli

The topic we are discussing now is about earning love, respect, relationships, and experiences along with money. Usually, when we talk about earning, the first thing that comes to mind is making money. I certainly wish for everyone to prosper, and I respect money as well. We must earn money, but that's not enough—we should manage it well, save it, and invest it wisely. Just as we respect money, we should also focus on earning love, respect, relationships, and experiences.

Speaking of experiences, I always emphasize the importance of *living in the moment.* That's why I say, *celebrate every moment—* which is exactly how we translate it into English. Why should we earn experiences? Because, as the saying goes, *take care of your moments, and moments will take care of you.* Let's hear what Tushar Nayak has to say about this topic.

Tushar Nayak

I truly appreciate today's topic—earning love, respect, relationships, and experiences along with money. In this world, nothing happens without money. People measure relationships based on money. Only those who understand the value of money can survive in this world, whether rich or poor.

Nowadays, people give more importance to money than to human beings. It is absolutely true that happiness cannot be bought with money. However, money has always held a significant place in society. People with money receive more respect, love, and recognition in relationships. Someone without money, regardless of their background, is often not valued much.

All relationships are built on financial stability—that is my perspective. If you want to maintain friendships, you need money. If you want to earn love and respect from family members, money is necessary. With that, I conclude my thoughts.

Samhita (Lecturer)

The topic being discussed today is *earning love, respect, relationships, and experiences along with money.* I would like to use the word *accumulate* instead of *earn.*

Setting money and experience aside for a moment, let's focus on love, respect, and relationships—these three are interconnected. To strengthen any relationship, love and mutual respect must be present. The foundation of these values is *trust*. If trust exists, relationships naturally thrive.

To maintain a strong relationship, we must be mindful of our words and actions. What does this mean? It means that when we speak, we should communicate in a way that does not hurt others. Additionally, any form of physical harm reduces love and respect. If you want a good relationship, be careful with how you treat people.

We should understand that the phrase is *"earning alongside money,"* not *"earning with money."* This means we must earn love, respect, and relationships just as we earn money. Life requires courage. Just as we strive to earn money, we must also strive to earn love and respect in society.

The more love we give, the more we receive. Love and respect do not require money. Isn't that true? Money is not necessary to show love or to respect someone.

Experiences, on the other hand, come naturally as we live each day. Money alone cannot buy experience. We can list experiences on a résumé, but real experience comes only to those who truly live through it. That is why they say, *"Life is the best teacher."* No one can teach us the lessons that life itself teaches.

So, along with money, earn these four things as well, because they cannot be bought with money. Thank you.

Katte Erriswamy

Today's topic—*earning love, respect, relationships, and experiences along with money*—is indeed thought-provoking.

Money can be earned in various ways. In today's online era, it is possible to earn money within an hour. There are countless ways to earn without much effort.

However, love and respect must be *preserved* once received. It is our responsibility to nurture and sustain them. That is why people say that *unasked-for respect is far greater than rewards received upon request.*

Similarly, experience is equally valuable. We learn best from the experiences of our elders. By observing them and listening to their stories, we can gain wisdom. Without experience, nothing is possible in life. That is my perspective.

Jayaprakash

Dear friends, money is important in life. Along with it, love, respect, relationships, and experiences are also crucial. Everyone already knows this, but when we discuss and reflect on such topics, it encourages deeper thinking.

Our goal is to spark thoughts that lead to transformation and inspiration through our words.

The Ultimate Truth of Life

Rakesh Jhunjhunwala's Final Words Before Passing Away (Net Worth: ₹45,000 Crore)

"In the business world, I reached the peak of success. Others considered my life a great achievement. However, beyond work, I found no real joy. Money was only a reality that I could use."

PERSONALITY MIRROR TRANSFORMS YOU

"As I lay in a hospital bed, looking back at my entire life, I realized that the fame and wealth I had once been proud of became meaningless and forgotten at the doorstep of death."

"You can hire people to drive your car or earn money for you. But you cannot hire someone to suffer or die in your place."

"Material things that are lost can be replaced. But one thing that, once lost, can never be found again is 'LIFE' itself."

"At every stage of life, we must remember that one day, our hearts will stop beating."

"Love your family, spouse, and friends... Take good care of them, never betray them, and never be dishonest."

"As we grow older and wiser, we realize that whether we wear a ₹300 watch or a ₹3,000,000 watch, both show the same time."

"Whether we have a wallet worth ₹100 or ₹500, the contents inside remain the same."

"Whether we drive a car worth ₹5 lakh or ₹50 lakh, the road and distance remain the same, and we reach the same destination."

"Whether we live in a 300-square-foot house or a 3,000-square-foot house, the loneliness inside remains the same."

"True inner happiness does not come from material possessions."

"Whether we fly first-class or economy, if the plane crashes, we all go down together."

"Therefore, the real happiness in life comes from having good friends, siblings, and loved ones with whom we can laugh, talk, sing, and share joy."

The Undeniable Truth of Life:

- *Do not raise your children to be rich. Instead, teach them to be happy. Then, when they grow up, they will understand the value of things, not just their price.*

Three Places That Teach the True Meaning of Life:

1. Hospital – Here, you realize that nothing is more valuable than health.
2. Jail – Here, you understand how precious freedom is.
3. Cemetery – Here, you learn that life is ultimately nothing.

"The ground we walk on today may not be ours tomorrow."

"Let us be humble and always be grateful for what we have."

7D.

SPEAK TO GET RICH

Shankar:
Hello, everyone.

My name is Shankar. I am a wealth coach. I provide coaching about the stock market, wealth, and money. Usually, you see Sir interviewing others. But today, let's give it a twist. I am going to interview him instead. We are going to put him in the spotlight and ask him some tough questions. Are you all ready? If you are ready, comment "Ready!"

Sir, welcome to your own show.

So, my first question—God has given you the gift of speech. Can one use their words to make money? If so, what are the different ways to do it?

Jayaprakash Nagathihalli: I used to do stage show anchoring. I was an anchor for ten years. I fondly remember working with Aparna. Back in the 90s, I did about 25 shows with her. Anchoring used to pay well. Before that, I was working in radio, where the pay was lower but still decent. Later, I was selected as an official newsreader on TV. The more news we read, the more we got paid. Then, I started conducting interviews, and we were allowed a maximum of ten per month. So, ten interviews multiplied by the payment per interview. That's how I earned money then. Later, I became a trainer, where speaking is an essential skill.

Shankar: So, words generate wealth.

Jayaprakash Nagathihalli: Yes! Nowadays, few are making up to ₹50,000 per day through training sessions.

Shankar: Oh my God! Okay.

Jayaprakash Nagathihalli: So, isn't it possible to earn through training?

Shankar: Definitely.

Jayaprakash Nagathihalli: Apart from that, I conduct online and offline classes. People attend my sessions not just to listen but to learn. However, some people hesitate to speak or share their knowledge. Since I am both a trainer and a mentor, I consider myself fortunate because I can quickly understand people's strengths and weaknesses. I have interviewed over 2,000 achievers and observed them closely. When someone sits in front of me, I can immediately gauge their strengths and weaknesses. By thinking positively, I have developed insights that others now call "divine power." At first, I was surprised, but then I started accepting it.

Shankar: But it's true! You have a glow on your face. I can see it.

Jayaprakash Nagathihalli: Thank you!

Shankar: It's not just the glow; it's something divine. I want to add a couple more points. Earlier, it was radio and TV. Now, it's the era of social media—YouTube, Instagram. Many people create YouTube videos about what they know, without needing anything else. They are earning well from it.

Jayaprakash Nagathihalli: I recently saw a news article about a lorry driver who makes ₹10 lakh per month just by making YouTube videos.

Shankar: Exactly! He shares information about how to drive a lorry, the procedures involved, and so on. This is proof that you can make money through speech. You just need to learn how to speak effectively. The choice of words matters, and so does the impact they create. If you want to learn, you should learn from experienced people. Sir is here!

Jayaprakash Nagathihalli: To put it simply—using the right words at the right time.

Shankar: Right words at the right time—perfect!

Jayaprakash Nagathihalli: It all starts with thoughts. I have a simple formula: The Three C's—Cool, Calm, and Comfortable.

Shankar: Wow!

Jayaprakash Nagathihalli: When you stay cool, calm, and comfortable, your thoughts become clear. Remove unwanted distractions. When thoughts are clear, they turn into words. And when you articulate them properly, they create an impact. Focus on what to say and what to leave out. Communication requires mental preparedness. Next is the power of words and language proficiency. Language is the vehicle of communication. Along with language, body language matters.

Now, if I just sit still, that's not engaging. But when I use gestures and maintain good posture, it makes a difference. Body language should be natural.

Your voice is another crucial factor. The pitch, tone, pace, and flow of your voice determine how powerful your speech is.

Shankar: Wow! Amazing insights.

Jayaprakash Nagathihalli: Yes! Your voice is the boss of your speech.

Shankar: Absolutely! Now, my next question—many youngsters today have technical skills like coding. But they struggle with communication, whether in a corporate setting or making videos. What advice would you give them?

Jayaprakash Nagathihalli: Communication is one of the ten essential life skills, and it is considered as the king of life skills. Why? Because 60–75% of your personality transformation happens through Communication Skills.

To improve communication, I suggest three inputs:

1. **Listening**
2. **Reading**
3. **Viewing**

Then, there are three outputs:

1. **Speaking**
2. **Writing**
3. **Body language**

I always say—your writing can shape your destiny.

Shankar: Wow! That's deep.

Jayaprakash Nagathihalli: There was a research article in *The Times of India* that said when you write with your hand, the nerves in your fingers send signals to your brain, reinforcing learning. So, write more! You can script your own future.

Shankar: That's incredible!

Jayaprakash Nagathihalli: Another crucial aspect is body language. I am not an astrologer, but by observing a person, I can understand their mindset. I can quickly assess whether someone is genuine or not. But I consciously switch off this ability in my daily life, or else it can get overwhelming.

Shankar: Wow!

Jayaprakash Nagathihalli: That's why I focus only on those who seek mentorship. Otherwise, seeing so many negative people can be exhausting. My goal, like yours, is to transform people into successful individuals and help them develop a magnetic personality.

Shankar: Yes!

Jayaprakash Nagathihalli: People should feel drawn toward you, take selfies with you, and even bow to you in respect—not because of external appearance but because of the energy and positivity you radiate.

Shankar: Absolutely!

Jayaprakash Nagathihalli: This is the power of positive thinking and affirmations. When you think positively, good things happen. When you master communication, you become a "money magnet."

Shankar: So true!

Let's revise once more for our viewers. What are the three inputs and three outputs of communication?

Jayaprakash Nagathihalli:

Inputs:

1. Listening
2. Reading
3. Viewing

Outputs:

1. Speaking
2. Writing
3. Body language

Shankar: That's powerful. If you integrate these into your life, your communication skills will automatically improve.

Jayaprakash Nagathihalli: Absolutely! I can even sign an autograph guaranteeing that you will succeed!

Shankar: So inspiring! Communication is not just about talking; it's about how effectively you connect with others.

Jayaprakash Nagathihalli: Yes, and the first level of communication is **"Me to Me"**—self-communication. It improves self-awareness. Then comes **"Me to You"**—speaking to others. And finally, **"You to Me"**—listening to others.

Shankar: That's gold! Thank you, sir, for this enlightening conversation.

Jayaprakash Nagathihalli:

No one was there to guide me back then. But now, I am here. If needed, I can share my 30 years of experience in just three days. But I didn't have that opportunity. I had to struggle, learn on my own, face challenges, and even endure criticism. Some people would say, *"Why do you keep bothering us?"*—especially when I used to go to Doordarshan in the beginning.

But do you know what makes me happy? The same people at Doordarshan later started recognizing me. K.S. Achyuthan, the news head, once said, *"Jayaprakash is like a prince of Doordarshan."*

Shankar: Oh my God!

Jayaprakash Nagathihalli: Girish Karnad called me *"a marvelous interviewer."* Sudha Murthy said, *"He is one of the best interviewers I have ever seen."* So over time, things changed. That's when I realized—if you put in the effort, you can achieve success.

I started learning more about public speaking and communication. I once attended a Jaycees Training Program and initially thought, *"What more can they teach me? I already know 95% of this!"* But I soon realized that the remaining 5% was extremely important. That realization made me more eager to learn.

From 1996 to 2004, I underwent various training programs, eventually becoming a State Trainer, National Trainer, and International Trainer. I even completed Excel Graduation and earned an International Trainer Certification from an American University.

Shankar: Oh my God! That's amazing.

Jayaprakash Nagathihalli: That's a brief journey of my training career. Eventually, I decided to leave my government job in 2008 and pursue training full-time. Now in 2024, I feel happier than ever. The recognition I have received, and most importantly, seeing people succeed after listening to my talks, gives me immense satisfaction.

Shankar: That's wonderful!

Jayaprakash Nagathihalli: I think I answered multiple questions at once.

Shankar: My next question is very important because many people have aspirations. Some want to become great speakers, some want to earn more money, and some want to achieve success. But they often have excuses like, *"I don't have exposure, I don't have anyone to guide me, I don't have support."*

So, in your life, how important were mentors, guides, and coaches? Can you share your thoughts on their role?

Jayaprakash Nagathihalli: When I qualified as an International Trainer in 2004, the other participants literally lifted me in the air in celebration!

Shankar: Oh my God!

Jayaprakash Nagathihalli: Because no one expected me to pass on the first attempt. The norm was that people took multiple attempts before qualifying. When I see that photo, it still surprises me.

One of my mentors, Sunil Kumar from Hyderabad, once gave me a life-changing piece of advice. I told him I was thinking of quitting my government job to become a full-time trainer, and he said: *"Jayaprakash, if you choose a different profession, someone else can copy what you do. But nobody can copy YOU. You are unique. Focus on your uniqueness, and the world will respect you."*

That motivated me a lot. Another mentor, Ravi Rohidekar, encouraged me by saying, *"You should become a trainer."* That support played a crucial role in my journey.

A mentor can refine and shape you, but for that, you must be open to correction.

Shankar: That's true!

Jayaprakash Nagathihalli: Many people get offended when they receive feedback. Some even leave online classes just because they don't like being corrected. I always believe in Assertive Communication—I teach this everywhere.

Shankar: Assertive communication is extremely important. Many people struggle with confidence, conviction, and clarity in communication. But if they learn this skill, they can confidently express what they want.

Jayaprakash Nagathihalli: Exactly! Assertive communication is like a mirror. If someone tells me, *"I don't like you,"* I smile and ask them, *"Why don't you like me?"* That way, they open up. It's all about the choice of words.

Shankar: Yes, raising your words instead of your voice makes a big difference.

Jayaprakash Nagathihalli: Absolutely! *"Raise your words, not your voice."* That applies in family life, workplaces, and even in relationships.

1. I categorize communication into four areas: Personal Growth – Helps in building confidence.
2. Family Relationships – Improves interactions with parents, children, and relatives.
3. Workplace – Helps in dealing with colleagues and superiors.
4. Society – Encourages people to be socially responsible.

Shankar: That makes so much sense! So, for someone who wants to improve their public speaking and leadership skills, you mentioned a three-day boot camp. Can you share more details?

Jayaprakash Nagathihalli: Yes! I conduct a three-day residential boot camp at a beautiful place near Devanahalli called The School of Ancient Wisdom. A German lady, Manize, created this 10-acre spiritual retreat, filled with trees, meditation spaces, and serene landscapes.

I have conducted seven workshops there already. The atmosphere itself helps in transformation. Unlike regular resorts, this place has a deep, spiritual energy. Many yogis have meditated there.

- During the camp: We have morning walks with informal learning sessions.
- We conduct intensive classes, sometimes until 10–11 PM.
- The connectivity between participants grows immensely.

People have seen a 25–50% transformation in just three days.

Shankar: Wow! That sounds amazing! So, who can attend this?

- **Jayaprakash Nagathihalli:** Anyone who wants to: Improve their communication skills.

- Become a leader.
- Achieve success in life.
- Develop expertise in their field.

This boot camp is ideal for professionals, entrepreneurs, and anyone who wants personal growth. It includes food, accommodation, and training.

For more details, call 9341259267.

Shankar: That's great! Now, you've interviewed many people and met numerous successful personalities. If someone wants personal development, what areas should they focus on?

1. **Jayaprakash Nagathihalli:** I break it down into six key aspects: Physical Health – Take care of your body because it's your biggest asset.
2. Mental Growth – Constantly learn and improve your knowledge.
3. Emotional Balance – Manage emotions effectively.
4. Social Skills – Build meaningful relationships.
5. Financial Stability – Learn to manage and grow your wealth.
6. Spiritual Connection – Have a sense of purpose and inner peace.

Shankar: That's an eye-opening perspective! Also, I love what you said about the body being the most valuable real estate on Earth. We invest in houses, flats, and properties but often neglect our own health.

Jayaprakash Nagathihalli: Exactly! Lately, I've started practicing meditation, and I can actually feel the energy flow within my body.

Shankar: That's incredible!

Jayaprakash Nagathihalli: I can feel the energy flowing throughout my body. That's why I have started developing a deeper sense of care for my body. Number 2 is the mind. *Mind your mind; mind will mind you.*

Shankar: Wow! *Mind your mind; mind will mind you.*

Jayaprakash Nagathihalli: The mind is like a parachute—it works only when it is open. So, open it up! Come to such training programs to open it up. Many people don't even use their minds properly; it just sits idle. They don't even realize that just as hunger is natural for the stomach, we must develop hunger for the brain too. I always say, "Feed your mind daily."

Then comes Intellectual Growth—sharpening the mind and making wise decisions. This helps with decision-making and problem-solving. Be a thinker! Not someone who just worries, but someone who analyzes situations thoughtfully.

Shankar: Wow!

Jayaprakash Nagathihalli: After intellectual growth comes emotional intelligence—the ability to experience and understand emotions. You and I are friends, but I can't say, *"I like Shankar Kulkarni as much as I like five crore rupees."*

Shankar: Got it.

Jayaprakash Nagathihalli: I can only feel it. Through words, support, or emotions. I can't quantify how much I love my mother in terms of money. Emotional intelligence is about things that cannot be captured in words but can only be felt. Pay attention to it. If you truly understand this, you will find happiness.

Shankar: True.

Jayaprakash Nagathihalli: This is the first important point.

Shankar: Yes.

Jayaprakash Nagathihalli: Emotional intelligence is key. Then comes spiritual personality—positivity. We are all human beings, but we must learn to be humane. It's about reducing negativity, increasing positivity, giving more, and being socially responsible. It's about developing a universal mindset where you see the whole world as yours. That is how you cultivate spiritual intelligence.

Then comes financial intelligence.

Shankar: Wow!

Jayaprakash Nagathihalli: You must learn to earn, save, and grow your wealth. Earn, save, and grow.

Shankar: Wow!

Jayaprakash Nagathihalli: When you keep doing these things, guides like us will help you understand where to invest and how to grow. It's about planting the seed, nurturing the plant, and later harvesting the fruits. Correct? Focus on the roots, and the fruits will come.

Shankar: The fruits will come.

Jayaprakash Nagathihalli: But most people don't focus on the roots. They only want to pick the fruits. But it doesn't work that way, and that's something I always emphasize.

Shankar: That is extremely important. Before I close, I have one last question. You spoke about roots and fruits. You once mentioned the bamboo tree example—can you share that with the audience? Because many people put in efforts, but they don't see results immediately, so they get discouraged. They don't realize that growth is happening inside. Please explain that.

Jayaprakash Nagathihalli: This is called the Musa Bamboo story. Do you know who first told me about it? Shrikanth Rao, the owner of Boyers Company. I once made a video on entrepreneurship with him, and hc shared this story. Shrikanth, thank you for teaching me this!

I recently shared this story at a conference as well. The Musa Bamboo works in a fascinating way. Once you plant its seed, for five years, it grows only underground, developing deep roots. Above the ground, there is no sign of growth at all. Then, after five years, it suddenly starts growing one foot per day—eventually reaching 500 feet high!

Shankar: Oh my God!

Jayaprakash Nagathihalli: So, no matter how much effort you put in today, it will definitely give you results tomorrow. I have witnessed this myself.

For example, look at how much knowledge Shankar Kulkarni has gained. We have attended workshops together, constantly learning from different places. Today, just like the Musa Bamboo, he has grown and is now interviewing me.

Before this interview, I shared this story with him, and now he is sharing it with you all—because he wants you to benefit from it too.

Shankar: I was so inspired by that story! And I don't want to keep that inspiration to myself—I want to share it with you all so that you can benefit too.

So, thank you so much! I have learned so many valuable ideas today—about personality development, communication, public speaking, input-output learning, and life as a whole. Life is not just about money. It's not just about the body. It's about overall well-being. You have given me a fantastic perspective. Thank you so much!

Jayaprakash Nagathihalli: Thank you! Shankar Kulkarni is a dear friend, and we will continue sharing such insights with all of you. Stay connected! I have my own YouTube channel, "Transformation Unlimited," and my organization's channel. So, subscribe to our YouTube channels.

Shankar: You must subscribe! And remember—subscribing is free! Don't forget to like the video as well—it doesn't cost anything.

When you like something, you spread good karma. If you do something good for others, someone else will do something good for you. So, don't hold back from liking, commenting, and sharing this with others.

Support sir's work. Thank you, Guruji!

Jayaprakash Nagathihalli: Thank you!

Shankar: Wonderful!

8.

Physical Mirror

Body

Do not belittle the body, my friend,
Do not look down upon it.
From the actions you have imagined,
Even if you call it a mere bundle of flesh,
It remains beautiful.
Every emotion and experience is a gift from it,
Even the most profound realizations arise from it.

As you read, you recite it like a sacred mantra,
A machine that toils on its own accord.
Yet, it bears your name,
Though it remains more obedient to nature than to you.

You use this ladder to climb,
And then you complain about its burden.
But once you leave the body behind,
What remains? Where is the connection then?

— B. R. Lakshman Rao

ಆರೋಗ್ಯ ಮತ್ತು ಫಿಟ್ನೆಸ್

Physical Personality

"YOUR BODY IS THE PERMANENT ADDRESS IN YOUR LIFE."

The significance of physical personality can be seen in many dimensions. It is related to a person's strength, health, and self-confidence. It helps enhance one's conduct, emotions, and presentation skills.

1. Self-confidence – A good physical personality instills greater self-confidence.
2. Health – A healthy body is the home of the soul. Taking care of one's physique through balanced nutrition and exercise ensures a good physical state. *Prevention is better than cure.*
3. Attractiveness – Physical personality leaves a lasting impression on others. Good posture, appropriate dressing, and body language enhance attractiveness. *Grooming – Pay attention to neatness and appearance.*
4. Social Influence – A well-maintained physical personality can help build strong social connections and influence.

Quotes from Great Achievers:

1. Mahatma Gandhi: *"Health is the greatest wealth."*
2. Aristotle: *"The health of the body is essential for mental strength."*
3. Bruce Lee: *"Personality is not limited to the size of the body or mind."*
4. Arnold Schwarzenegger: *"The body must be refined through discipline. The power of the mind should align with the strength of the body."*
5. Swami Vivekananda: *"Self-confidence is the source of strength; maintaining a strong body ensures a sound mind and heart."*

Lifestyle Habits to Maintain Physical Health:

1. Balanced Nutrition – A nutritious and well-balanced diet is the foundation of good physical health. Fruits, vegetables, whole grains, protein, and healthy fats should be a part of daily meals.
2. Regular Exercise – At least 30 minutes of physical activity daily helps regulate body weight and improves heart health. *Enjoy the pain!*
3. Healthy Sleep – Adequate rest is essential for physical recovery. Sleeping 6 to 8 hours every night is recommended.
4. Hydration – Drinking at least 8 glasses of water daily is crucial for maintaining a healthy body.
5. Avoiding Harmful Substances – Stay away from excessive alcohol, smoking, and harmful drugs.

By incorporating these habits into daily life, one can maintain physical well-being and ensure long-term health.

8A.

Personality Development Through Sports

Arjun Devayya

Jayaprakash Nagathihalli: Good morning! Hello friends, a warm welcome to the phone-in program. Dear viewers, sports activate human beings and also serve as a path to complete happiness. To explain how sports contribute to personality development, we have with us Arjun Devayya, a nine-time national champion in athletics, a silver medalist in the Asian Athletics Championships, and a gold medalist in the South Asian

Games. Arjun Devayya, a warm welcome to our phone-in program.

Arjun Devayya: Namaste, sir.

Jayaprakash Nagathihalli: Arjun Devayya, since you have been deeply involved in sports, what is the significance of sports?

Arjun Devayya: First of all, my heartfelt regards to all the viewers. The importance of sports is immense. To put it simply, engaging in sports helps us maintain good physical health. More importantly, it serves as a foundation for friendship and camaraderie. Many people tend to think that sports are only about competing at the international, national, or state level and showcasing one's talent. But sports are not just limited to that.

Socrates beautifully expressed this idea: *"What a disgrace it is for a man to grow old without seeing the beauty of the strength of his body."* This means that every individual must realize how capable their body is and how well it can perform. Sports provide a broad-minded perspective, instill courage, and build self-confidence.

However, viewers should not misunderstand and think that everything can be achieved only through sports. Academics and education hold primary importance, and children must give them due attention. But alongside academics, sports are crucial because they help bring out one's inner potential and nurture essential attitudes. That is why I prefer to call it a *sports activity* rather than just sports.

Jayaprakash Nagathihalli: So, following what you said, can we conclude that sports play a role in personality development?

Arjun Devayya: Absolutely! Let me share a brief example from my life. I was born and raised in a village, studied in a Kannada-medium school, and later moved to the city. Until my final year of B.Com, I had never engaged in any extracurricular activities. I had a good circle of friends and remained within that comfort zone. I hesitated to interact with others beyond my group.

However, during my final year, I realized that I could participate in sports. Once I started, I noticed a transformation within myself. Today, even in front of thousands of people, I can speak without any hesitation. The self-consciousness and fear of interaction I once had disappeared entirely.

There's a saying that no wisdom or advice truly applies to someone until they experience it themselves. Similarly, unless one actively participates in something, it is difficult to explain its impact to others. That is why I firmly believe that personality development through sports is something people must experience firsthand.

Jayaprakash Nagathihalli: So, even without realizing it, sports help people build self-confidence?

Arjun Devayya: Absolutely, yes!

Jayaprakash Nagathihalli: How does that happen?

Arjun Devayya: When we engage in any physical activity, physiological changes occur within us. These metabolic changes make us more active. If a person is physically agile, it means their body is well-conditioned.

Similarly, when you engage in sports, you gradually build confidence. You start believing, *"Yes, I can do this!"* Over time, sports instill courage, determination, and assurance within us. That confidence is not something someone can simply give you—you have to experience it.

That's why I encourage viewers to engage in sports activities systematically. Once they do, they will feel a noticeable change within themselves. They will become more energetic throughout the day, and this energy will help them perform their tasks more efficiently.

Jayaprakash Nagathihalli: You're saying that someone who once hesitated to talk to others can gain the confidence to speak in front of thousands?

Arjun Devayya: Yes, exactly!

Jayaprakash Nagathihalli: How does sports cultivate this kind of courage to face situations, even difficult ones?

Arjun Devayya: Initially, many people fear speaking on a stage. They think, *"Oh no! I'm scared to talk!"* But in sports, when you interact with numerous people daily, you naturally become comfortable. This interaction isn't something you consciously force yourself to do—it just happens.

In contrast, if you join a public speaking course to overcome stage fear, you approach it with self-consciousness. But in sports, you meet and interact with people naturally, whether while playing, walking, or engaging in activities. This daily interaction gradually eliminates fear. One day, you'll find yourself speaking confidently in front of a crowd without hesitation.

Jayaprakash Nagathihalli: We often hear the term *sportive spirit*—the sportsmanship attitude. If someone regularly plays sports, can they maintain that sportsmanship in life? How does it shape their personality?

Arjun Devayya: Not all athletes automatically have a broad-minded sportsman spirit, but many do. Since they frequently experience wins and losses, they learn to accept them with a balanced mindset.

Athletes often develop a straightforward and open attitude. However, I want to clarify the difference between *sports activities* and *being an athlete*. A sports activity is something everyone can engage in, whereas an athlete is someone who pursues sports as a profession.

When you engage in sports activities, you become more open-minded and willing to share and collaborate. You start appreciating different perspectives and experiences. Sports naturally expose you to diverse people, cultures, and ways of thinking, making you more adaptable and understanding.

Jayaprakash Nagathihalli: We live in a competitive era. People have to keep up with competition in every field. Since sports involve competition, does playing sports help develop a competitive mindset?

Arjun Devayya: There is a difference between *sportive spirit* and *competitive spirit*. You may have heard the saying, *"Everything is fair in love and war."* Similarly, in a sports arena, an opponent is like a rival, even if they are a friend outside the game.

PERSONALITY MIRROR TRANSFORMS YOU

This creates a *friendly rivalry*—both players want to win. This is what we call *competitive spirit*. However, the competition is healthy, and there is no ill will involved. Unlike war, where the goal is destruction, sports competition is about showcasing one's ability while maintaining respect for the opponent.

After the game, the rivalry ends, and players become friends again. That is the difference between competitive spirit and sportsmanship.

Jayaprakash Nagathihalli: You emphasize that sports help reduce shyness and hesitation. Do you think these qualities are widespread among people? If someone participates in sports, can they develop a more open and broad-minded attitude?

Arjun Devayya: Definitely! That's why I always say, I am not speaking from theory or comparison—I speak from personal experience. I was once hesitant and shy, but sports changed me.

Anyone who actively engages in sports will experience personal growth, increased confidence, and a broader perspective. Whether it's communication, teamwork, resilience, or discipline, sports play a significant role in shaping one's personality.

Jayaprakash Nagathihalli: So, you're saying that they create that situation themselves.

Arjun Devayya: You've put it very aptly. They create the situation.

Jayaprakash Nagathihalli: And mentally, they become stronger in a way.

Arjun Devayya: Yes.

Jayaprakash Nagathihalli: How does that happen?

Arjun Devayya: What I mentioned earlier is that when someone engages in sports activities, certain physical—biological—changes occur in them. Physical development also takes place. Through this change, they can develop resilience. When you put in your optimum level of effort, you gain a sense of strength and confidence. I had used the word 'confidence' before. When confidence develops in a person, you can see it on their face—it is evident in their demeanor. They have clarity and direction in what they do.

However, I want to make a subtle point here, especially for athletes and those who are watching. Simply playing sports does not automatically develop all these qualities. Along with sports, one must cultivate the right attitude—it is like the icing on the cake. If not, I have seen many athletes who are quite rough in their behavior. When they behave rudely, others tend to say, "Look at these athletes, how rough they are."

So, it is essential to develop a well-rounded personality. That's why I said education plays a major role. You need to cultivate the right attitude. True resilience is a blend of both—sports and education. The saying goes, "A sound mind in a sound body." There needs to be balance. When this balance exists, resilience naturally follows. If we think resilience is just about being firm or daring in speech, it doesn't work that way.

Jayaprakash Nagathihalli: So, it must be developed positively...

Arjun Devayya: Yes, it must be developed positively.

Jayaprakash Nagathihalli: Now, let's focus on children. How does engaging in such activities benefit them?

Arjun Devayya: That's a very important question, Jayaprakash. I'd like to share a message with my parents here. Many parents today focus solely on academics. As soon as children reach eighth grade, parents start worrying about exams. Ninth grade, tenth grade—it's all about studies. The moment they enter tenth grade, they are sent for tuition. After tenth, it's PUC, then CET. They are constantly chasing marks—99%, 100%. But I want to make an important point: scoring 99% or 100% alone does not create a complete individual.

I've observed that many young children today lack body language. They appear physically weak, lacking courage, resilience, and self-confidence. This is because their biological development has not taken place properly. Many children today are playing sports only on computers, sitting indoors.

Jayaprakash Nagathihalli: So, do they watch more and play less?

Arjun Devayya: Yes, they play on computers instead of on the field. For example, instead of playing basketball on the ground, they are playing it on a computer screen. They need to go out and sweat it out. Another issue is that many schools today do not even have playgrounds. Parents are only concerned about studies, asking, "Why is my child not excelling in academics?" Schools also focus entirely on studies, ignoring physical development.

As a result, children do not develop self-confidence. They grow up with a restricted mindset, becoming like cattle walking in a straight line without questioning anything. This is not how it should be. There should be balanced development. Parents may ask, "Where is the time for all this?" But I'd like to remind them of Thomas Alva Edison. His mother, who was a teacher, personally educated him when his school dismissed him as a weak student. She nurtured him to the level where he became one of the greatest scientists, inventing over 1,100 things!

So, parents need to think beyond marks. Sports are not a waste of time. If children cut down on some unnecessary social activities, they can find time for both studies and sports. Either the child should go to school, or the school should come home.

Jayaprakash Nagathihalli: Let's take a call. Mr. Nagaraj is calling. Nagaraj, sir, namaste.

Nagaraj: Sir, my name is Subedar Nagaraj. I am very happy to be watching this program.

Jayaprakash Nagathihalli: Please ask your question.

Arjun Devayya: You, too, are an athlete, Nagaraj sir. Because everyone in the army is protecting our nation, just like sports promote teamwork and unity. Please go ahead with your question.

Nagaraj: Sir, I really appreciate this program. My question is—

Arjun Devayya: Yes, sir, please go ahead.

Nagaraj: More such programs should be conducted.

Arjun Devayya: Absolutely, sir.

Nagaraj: Also, every week, there should be a program featuring sports personalities who have contributed to the nation.

Arjun Devayya: Sir, I have appeared on DD Chandana multiple times for such programs, and they continue to organize them. They are keen on creating awareness and will certainly take note of your suggestion. Do you have any other topic-related questions?

Nagaraj: Yes, in our army...

Jayaprakash Nagathihalli: Hold on. If he continues his question, I want to return to the discussion on children.

Arjun Devayya: Yes.

Jayaprakash Nagathihalli: In any country, the youth play a crucial role.

Arjun Devayya: Absolutely.

Jayaprakash Nagathihalli: How does sports directly impact young people?

Arjun Devayya: We always say that the youth are the future of the nation. Today's youth are tomorrow's responsible citizens. But this is not just about education. Education is primary, no doubt. However, if young people are not physically strong, how will they face challenges? Parents and teachers need to ensure balanced development.

Take, for example, former US President George Bush. He was an avid runner and marathon participant. In one of his interviews, he said, "My day starts at 6 AM with exercise. When I reach the office, I expect everyone to be there already." He made fitness a priority and emphasized, "If I, as the President of the United States, can find time for physical activity, then everyone can."

Jayaprakash Nagathihalli: We have a call from Bijapur. Suresh is on the line. Namaste, Suresh.

Suresh: I want to ask about stage courage. I have tried going on stage a few times, but I get nervous and struggle.

Arjun Devayya: Got it, Suresh. Though this is not directly related to sports, it is indirectly connected. I was just like you once. In my B.Com final year, I couldn't speak for even a minute on stage. My advice is to keep trying. Start with small programs and build confidence. Keep practicing, and you will succeed.

Suresh: Okay.

Arjun Devayya: Thank you, Suresh, for calling.

Jayaprakash Nagathihalli: We were talking about youth, but after youth comes old age.

Arjun Devayya: Yes, sir.

Jayaprakash Nagathihalli: In old age, people often feel like life is coming to an end. What is your message to them?

Arjun Devayya: Sports and physical activity help keep our muscles active. When muscles are toned, aging slows down. There is a theory—"use and disuse." What you use develops; what you don't use deteriorates. Regular physical activity prevents muscle dysfunction, increasing longevity and keeping you energetic. That's why army personnel, even in old age, look fit and youthful.

Jayaprakash Nagathihalli: So, overall, irrespective of whether we win awards or receive recognition, engaging in activities that bring inner happiness is important?

Arjun Devayya: Absolutely. One must first do things for personal satisfaction. If you achieve something, it's an added bonus. If not, there's no need to be disappointed. As Mankuthimma's *Kagga* says... (continues with a quote).

Jayaprakash Nagathihalli: Along with modernity, do sports also provide a platform to enhance creativity?

Arjun Devayya: Absolutely! Many people talk about creativity, saying that you have to use both sides of your brain. But to use both sides of your brain effectively, you must engage your entire body. Sports is the best way to do this. When you participate in sports, you engage all your muscles, your entire muscle constitution, and your body constitution. If you want your creativity and intellectual brain to function optimally, you need to be balanced.

Jayaprakash Nagathihalli: That was very well explained. Even athletes who play sports still do exercises regularly.

Arjun Devayya: Yes.

Jayaprakash Nagathihalli: Some people cannot play sports due to lack of time. But exercise, at the very least, is essential, isn't it?

Arjun Devayya: Absolutely! I'd like to share a message with our viewers: When exercising, please don't just do it in your own way without proper guidance. There is a correct way to exercise. It must be done systematically. You need to know which muscles to stretch, how to stretch them, how much warm-up is required. Without a proper warm-up, some people stretch incorrectly and end up with injuries—sometimes permanent ones.

You also need to consider what kind of shoes to wear, their purpose, and many other factors. It's impossible to cover everything in one discussion. But one thing is certain—if you are not an expert in something, seek guidance from those who are. Learn the correct way to do things. Otherwise, in an attempt to do something beneficial, you might end up harming yourself. It's crucial not to do things incorrectly. Your body is not something to take for granted.

Jayaprakash Nagathihalli: Finally, what message would you like to give our viewers?

Arjun Devayya: Everything I've said so far—I urge you to implement it in your life. Sports will keep you energetic, and your daily routine will improve significantly. If needed, we can even prove this to you!

I work at the State Bank of India, where most of us have desk jobs. As an officer, I often talk to my colleagues and seniors about stress management. And I firmly believe that stress levels can be significantly reduced through physical activity.

One important thing I'd like to say to everyone: Take some time out of your daily schedule for exercise. If you don't, you may have to spend a lot more time later in hospitals and with doctors. That's my simple advice.

Jayaprakash Nagathihalli: That's an excellent and valuable piece of advice. Arjun Devayya, you've shared a lot of insightful information about how sports contribute to personality development and help individuals grow. Thank you very much for this discussion. Namaste.

Arjun Devayya: Many thanks, Jayaprakash! My heartfelt gratitude to everyone at DD Chandana. Namaste.

9.

Moving into Action

So far in this book, you have read about several inspiring aspects. Now, it's time to take action. Here are some suggestions to guide you:

1. PHYSICAL WELL-BEING

- Be with Nature – Spend time in nature.
- Exercise – Make exercise a regular habit.
- Acupressure – Try acupressure therapy.
- Massage – Get massages periodically.

2. MENTAL WELL-BEING

- Meditation is a must – Make meditation a daily practice.
- Pranayama – Practice breath control techniques.
- Be a continuous learner – Keep learning throughout life.
- Mind Your Mind; Mind Will Mind You – Always be aware of your thoughts.

3. INTELLECTUAL WELL-BEING

- Reading – Develop a reading habit.
- Writing – Express yourself through writing.
- Be a Problem Solver – Focus on finding solutions.
- Take Decisions – Make well-thought-out decisions.

- Make the Best Choices – Choose wisely in all aspects of life.

4. EMOTIONAL WELL-BEING

- Spread Happiness – Share joy with others.
- Adjust to Circumstances – Adapt to different situations.
- Respect Parents, Teachers & Seniors – Show gratitude and respect to elders.

5. SPIRITUAL WELL-BEING

- Practice Gratitude – Be thankful for what you have.
- Be Good & Do Good – Engage in good deeds and build a positive reputation.
- Being Human – Show compassion and kindness.
- Art of Giving – Develop a generous mindset.

6. FINANCIAL WELL-BEING

- Earn Well – Work hard and earn responsibly.
- Save Wisely – Manage your finances smartly.
- Invest More – Make strategic investments.
- Active & Passive Income – Establish multiple sources of income.

Your life is like a 6-wheel drive, and you are the DRIVER. Make sure to steer in the right direction! 🚀

10.

Towards Balance

Achieving balance in life is crucial. By integrating six key aspects of personality development with four special elements, life gains structure and clarity. Research and studies confirm that following this approach brings a unique charm to life.

1. PERSONAL ASPECTS

You are the most important person in your life. Prioritize yourself before anything else. Many people sacrifice their well-being by prioritizing others, which can lead to dissatisfaction. Understand yourself better, acquire the knowledge and skills you need, and engage in positive activities that enhance your mindset.

2. FAMILY ASPECTS

After yourself, your next priority should be your family. Your family is an extended version of yourself. The values upheld within a family shape its strength and unity. By experiencing different roles within the family and fostering loving relationships, you create a harmonious and fulfilling environment.

ಪಾತ್ರ

3. PROFESSIONAL ASPECTS

Your profession is like an extended family. Whether you are an entrepreneur, government employee, private sector worker, or freelancer, every career path offers unique experiences. Understanding and embracing these differences allows for a better professional and personal life balance.

4. SOCIAL ASPECTS

Every individual is a part of society. Building meaningful relationships within the community fosters personal growth. People who engage in altruistic acts earn the highest respect in society. Support those in need whenever possible, and let gratitude be the foundation of your life. When you give to society, it will support you in return.

By giving equal importance to these four aspects, life gains meaning and depth, leading to a fulfilling existence.

LIFE IS A BALANCING ACT.

★★★★

11.

MENTORING - The Light of Guidance

"The only way to make a nation great is to make its people great."

– Sir M. Visvesvaraya

These words highlight how essential it is to uplift people. Many individuals from different fields must come together to achieve this goal. Many successful individuals agree that mentoring can be a powerful remedy.

"Progress is not enough; one must aim for elevation."

– K.S. Nissar Ahmed

Achieving progress is essential, but aspiring for greater heights is even more crucial. Understanding the present situation and setting goals for continuous improvement is necessary. Knowledge, attitude, skills, and habits contribute significantly to this growth. Focusing on these four aspects is essential for success.

"Without guidance, the path is unclear;
Without a clear path, the goal is unreachable."

– Khalandar

These words by Khalandar emphasize the importance of having clarity in our journey before setting goals. A clear sense of direction is a fundamental requirement for success.

We must continually refine our lives and test ourselves. Mentorship acts as an accelerator. A mentor can guide you from where you are to where you want to be. They help you realize that you are your own competition. Research shows that only 10% of people truly live the life they desire. These individuals progress ten times faster than others. Thus, mentorship can change your trajectory.

Through mentorship, you can develop practical skills and refine the abilities you need. Every successful individual has had a mentor. If you do not spread your wings, you will never know how high you can soar. Mentors do not just provide knowledge; they awaken the hidden potential within you.

If you aspire to succeed, seek a mentor. Learn to value their experience and time. Be generous in reciprocating their guidance. Mentors help save your most precious resource—time. They do not make decisions for you; instead, they inspire you to make your own decisions.

Identify experts in your field and seek their guidance. Absorb their wisdom and experiences. Remember, the best investment you can make is in yourself.

Notable Quotes:

- Masti Venkatesha Iyengar:

"Do not sit idle, do not stop, do not descend; keep ascending."

BENEFITS OF PERSONALITY DEVELOPMENT & TRANSFORMATION TRAINING FROM JAYAPRAKASH NAGATHIHALLI:

1. Boost in Self-Confidence
2. Assertive Communication Skills
3. Mindset Transformation
4. Clarity of Goals
5. Emotional Stability
6. Problem-Solving Skills
7. Leadership Skills
8. Self-Development
9. Inner Peace

Improving one's personality also helps maintain inner peace and balance, paving the way for overall success.

HIGHLIGHTS OF Jayaprakash Nagathihalli & Transformation Unlimited YOUTUBE CHANNEL:

1. Personality Development & Mentorship – Insights on stress management, confidence-building, and problem-solving.
2. Inspirational Style – Real-life experiences and practical approaches that motivate people to face daily challenges.
3. Authentic Kannada Presentation – Simple and relatable language that reaches people of all ages.
4. Workshops & Training Sessions – Information on personality development classes and career training, helpful for students and professionals alike.

His resources provide guidance from career growth to personal development, enriching both knowledge and personality.

EXPERT OPINIONS ON JAYAPRAKASH NAGATHIHALLI:

- Justice Shivaraj V. Patil(Former Supreme Court Judge):
  "A great speaker, writer, and personality development coach. True knowledge is not stored in the mind; it must be shared with society."
- Dr. D.S. Vishwanath (Retd. IAS Officer):
  "Among great names in personality development like Dale Carnegie, Anthony Robbins, and Stephen Covey, in Kannada, Jayaprakash Nagathihalli is a respected and commendable name."
- G.S. Sridhar, Tumkur:
  "After living with self-doubt for 38 years, J.P. Sir helped me overcome it in just one hour."
- Dr. Amritaraj, Veterinary Officer, Harihara:
  "J.P. Sir has the magical ability to correct and refine individuals."
- Geetha, State President, Kannada Nadu Welfare Forum:
  "He is the only person who answers our questions with clarity and wisdom."

- Niranjan Gowda, Real Estate Entrepreneur:
  "Learning from a mentor like you is a blessing. Your guidance brings confidence, positivity, and prosperity."

ಅಪರಿಮಿತ ಪರಿವರ್ತನೆ
ಜಯಪ್ರಕಾಶ್ ನಾಗತಿಹಳ್ಳಿ

About The Author

JAYAPRAKASH NAGATHIHALLI

- Transformation MENTOR
- International TRAINER
- Best Selling AUTHOR
- Social Media INFLUENCER
-

Email: smilingjp@gmail.com

Mobile: +91 9886081188

————————————

TRAINER

- International Trainer
- 30+ years of rich training experience
- Trained over 10 Lakhs people so far.
- Online: Silver, Gold, Diamond & Platinum Modules
- Offline: ONE DAY & THREE DAYS Workshops

- Associated with many reputed Educational Institutions, Government, Private, Corporate and NGO's .

————————

SPECIALIZATION

Public Speaking
Communication / Life Skills
Personality Development etc.,
Customized Training Workshops

————————

AUTHOR OF KANNADA BOOKS

1. Nudigannadi
2. Solugalige Anjadiri
3. Keelarime
4. Anukshana Anubhavisi
5. Udyoga Koushalyagalu
6. Tiruvugala Arivu
7. Ananyate Ariyiri
8. Sadhakara Chandana
9. Sahitya Chandana
10. Vyaktitva Chandana
11. Nirupane Rirupisi
12. Jeevanothsaha
13. Lifu Namdene
14. Vyaktitva Darpana
15. Vyaktitva Parivartane
16. Tarabetiya Takattu

————————

BOOKS IN ENGLISH LANGUAGE

1. Fear Not Failures
2. Inferiority Complex
3. Celebrate Every Moment

4. Transform Your Life Instantly
5. Unlock the Power of Uniqueness
6. Personality Mirror Transforms You

——————————

VIDEOS ON

1. Humour
2. Examination
3. Failures to Success
4. Overcome Inferiority Complex
5. Be Happy
6. Be an Entrepreneur
7. Positive Attitude
8. Speech is Pearl
9. Enthusiasm
10. Turning Point
11. Unwanted
12. Art of Parenting

——————————

AUDIOS ON

1. Personality Development
2. Time Management
3. Melody of Life
4. Self Confidence
5. Short Poems
6. Happy Married Life

[Audios & Videos produced by Nagamma Foundation (R)
- Please Call +91 934 125 9267 to purchase Soft Copies]

——————————

SOCIAL MEDIA INFLUENCER

YOUTUBE CHANNELS
- Jayaprakash Nagathihalli & Transformation Unlimited - Over 55,000 SUBSCRIBERS

———————————

CONTINUOUS MOTIVATION & TRANSFORMATION
THROUGH VARIOUS TOPICS.
Uploaded more than 5,000 Videos till date.

———————————

ENTREPRENEUR

Proprietor, Transformation Unlimited

———————————

PHILANTHROPIST

Founder, Nagamma Foundation ®
GRATITUDE FUNCTION
- Recognized more than 200 achievers till this year.

———————————

PAST EXPERIENCES – ORGANIZER

Overall organized more than 500 cultural and literary
programmes for the community.
1. President, Youth Writers & Artists Guild - 10 years.
2. President, Junior Chamber International &
Zone Officer for 1 + 2 years.
3. Indo-Soviet Cultural Society
4. Karnataka State Peace & Solidarity Organization
5. Program Committee Member, Bharatiya Vidya Bhavan

MEDIA TV HOST

Anchored programmes on Chandana TV, Bangalore Doordarshan and interviewed more than 1,500 personalities for Television.
News reader for 3 years.

———————

RADIO

Presented more than 300 Radio programmes for Bangalore All India Radio.
Presented the Talk Series 'Solugalige Anjadiri'[FEAR NOT FAILURES] for Radio City FM.
Presented motivational series for Jnanavani FM.

———————

STAGE SHOWS

Anchored more than 1,000 programmes.

———————

ACTING

Acted in dramas, serials and movies.

———————

KARATE

Trained by Dr.A.K. Atre, Former Principal,
Vijaya College, Black Belt Holder trained for 4 years.

———————

WORKING TOWARDS PASSION

Gave up job in the Commercial Tax Department and became a full-time trainer in 2008.

———————————

QUALIFICATION

Science - Arts - Commerce - Training.
1. B.Sc., from Bangalore University.
2. Masters Degree in Mass Communication & Journalism & Diploma in Journalism
3. Diploma in Business Administration- 3 years
4. Excel Graduation from JCI University USA.

———————————

AWARDS

- Best District Youth Award
- Best Trainer of the year Award - Gurupuraskar
- Motivational Guru Award
- Super Achiever
- World Best Citizen Award
- Dr. Ambedkar Ratna Award
- Chanakya Award
- Sir M. Vishweshwaraiah Award
- Honoured by more than 1000 organizations
- Karnataka Rajyotsava Award by U CAN V CAN

———————————

VISION

- To train 2 million people.
- Be a Mentor for more achievers.

- To write more books.
- To inspire and transform through meaningful content on social media.
- Creating more Online Courses

Disclaimer